THE STEPHEN BECHTEL FUND

IMPRINT IN ECOLOGY AND THE ENVIRONMENT

The Stephen Bechtel Fund has

established this imprint to promote

understanding and conservation of

our natural environment.

The publisher gratefully acknowledges the generous contribution to this book provided by the Stephen Bechtel Fund.

THE FISH IN THE FOREST

Photographs by Doc White

Text by Dale Stokes

UNIVERSITY OF CALIFORNIA PRESS

Berkeley   Los Angeles   London

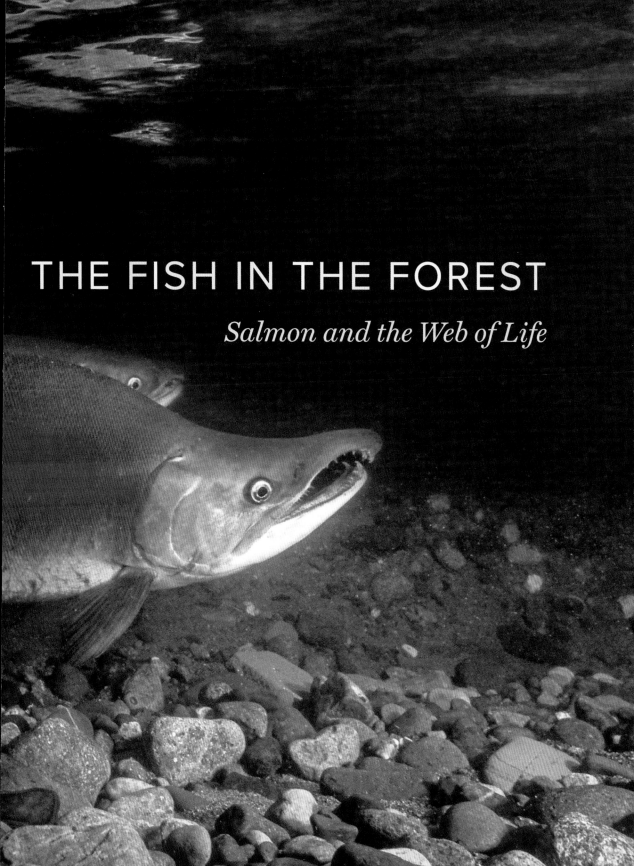

THE FISH IN THE FOREST

Salmon and the Web of Life

1 THE FOREST
AND THE FISH

27 LIFE AND DEATH
OF A SALMON

69 THE SALMON
SIGNATURE

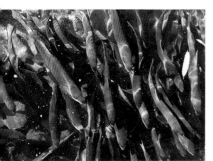

CONTENTS

81 SALMON
GESTALT

103 THE SALMON
FOREST

125 FULL
CIRCLE

147 ACKNOWLEDGMENTS

149 REFERENCES

THIS STORY begins and ends with a fish. That is to say, it begins and ends with a salmon, a fish that so dominates its coastal marine and terrestrial environment that the entire landscape of the north Pacific coast of North America may be considered the Salmon Forest. This story begins and ends with a fish, but along the way the story of the Salmon Forest touches on all the life of the temperate rain forest: the trees and shrubs, the algae in the rivers and streams, the birds and bears and bugs, the bacteria in the soil, the whales, otters, and seals, and the other fishes that live offshore. It is the story of an extremely complex ecosystem. When the molecules of what was once a salmon find their way to the tops of trees and into the flesh of animals far removed from the ocean, rivers, and streams where the salmon once swam, and when the actions of the salmon themselves can be seen to shape the very landscape on scales that span hundreds of kilometers and thousands of years, it becomes very difficult to distinguish where the salmon begins or ends from the point where it transforms into something entirely different. So the story of the Salmon Forest is a story of the interconnectedness of the sea and land and a fish that has evolved and become entwined in a landscape, a story that serves as a metaphor for all of life on earth.

o o o

WHAT IS A FISH? Fishes are difficult to define conveniently because for nearly every potential defining characteristic there seems to be an exception. And this difficult-to-classify group of animals contains half the number of vertebrates on earth; nearly 30,000 species, in 445 families, living almost everywhere, from the tropics to the poles. An ichthyologist roughly defines a fish as an *aquatic poikilothermic vertebrate* possessing *gills* throughout its life and having *fin*-shaped limbs, if it has any at all. This gross definition includes all water-living (aquatic), back-boned (vertebrate) animals with a fluctuating internal body temperature (poikilothermic), specialized tissues that can extract oxygen from water and excrete carbon dioxide (gills), and paddle-like structures for moving through a fluid (fins). Hence the large number of fish that are "fish."

The exceptions to this convenient piscine definition are spectacular examples of evolutionary adaptation. There are fish that spend the majority of their lives out of the water, with organs that have modified into primitive lungs; fish without fins at all, or fins that allow an ambulatory stroll as feet; and fish with fins that have transformed into a bewildering array of appendages like lures, claws, and spiky plumes. There are fish that lack bony skeletons, having only cartilage; and there are some fast-swimming pelagic species that maintain a body temperature that is warmer than the surrounding sea. Fish provide magnificent proof that given time and evolutionary natural selection, almost anything is possible. Adult fish range in size from less than a centimeter to more than fifteen meters in length. They can weigh anywhere from a few grams to dozens of tons. There are fish that make sounds, produce light in special organs, or secrete incredibly toxic venoms, and there are fish that can generate powerful jolts of electricity. Some fish can perform almost magical transformations in shape, color, or sex. They can live in the swiftest rivers, at the bottom of the ocean, under the polar ice, deep inside caves, or as parasites on others. And there are fish that can fly, or at least soar like birds.

So what then is a salmon? On the fourth day of his loving exposition on the sport and art of fishing, the piscator of Izaak Walton's *Compleat Angler* expounds nobly on the Atlantic salmon as the "King of Fish," for reasons that go beyond the fact that the art of catching the salmon of the British Isles was a sport cherished by nobleman and peasant alike. Here was a creature that migrated yearly by the hundreds of thousands up from the ocean to the highest streams. The salmon performed staggering feats of endurance and strength, leaping obstacles in their path, during their tireless upstream quest to spawn. They were fickle and difficult to catch with a cast hook or fly, but fought strongly when they did bother to bite, and they were blessed, or cursed, with succulent orange-red flesh. Even four centuries ago, the close ties between the presence of the salmon and the nature of the surrounding British landscape, Walton's "clear and sharp streams," were evident. Despite rules and regulations for the protection of the salmon, the decline in the quality of their habitat concomitant with the rise of industrialization led to a decline in their numbers. They were unable to adapt to a landscape increasingly and rapidly dominated by human society. Walton's streams, once choked with the bright, leaping, kingly fish, are now just a dream and a memory.

In the north Pacific, the salmon was, and still is, a central character in a coastal landscape that has been sustaining aboriginal peoples for thousands of years. The salmon, and hence, the Salmon Forest, provided wealth and security and was revered by widespread salmon-based cultures that ringed the north Pacific. In comparison, it is only relatively recently that the Salmon Forest has been subjected to the activities of commercial fishing empires and a competing, ever-growing complex of industries capitalizing on the wide range of natural resources present in the Pacific Northwest's marine and terrestrial environment. And it has only been more recently still that we have had the tools and motivation to tease apart the complexities of the Salmon Forest ecosystem. The question remains whether or not we can learn from previous ecological mistakes and fruitfully apply this new knowledge—which is ironically analogous to the mythology and wisdom of the salmon culture of North America's First Nation peoples—and preserve not just the salmon but the forest as well.

o   o   o

WHEN WE ALLUDE to the Salmon Forest, we refer to a terrestrial landscape that covers an enormous coastal region stretching from California north through British Columbia and Alaska, encircling thousands of offshore islands, and extending across the Bering Sea and along the coast of Russia to Japan and Korea. This coastal zone includes all those watersheds in which Pacific salmon have swum and spawned. These rivers and streams can penetrate thousands of kilometers into the interior of the continents, and because, as we shall see, the influence of the salmon can extend far beyond the banks of a stream, the real Salmon Forest covers an area much larger than we might expect.

This region encompasses a staggering variety of climates, terrains, and ecological habitats. It includes the volcanic slopes of the Cascade Mountains and the mighty Rockies, as well as coastal wetlands, grassy plateaus, alpine deserts, and Arctic tundra. It contains thousands of bays, islands, and estuaries. Its watersheds include lakes, streams, and rivers large and small, from gushing torrents to tiny seasonal rivulets. The climate varies enormously over such a large area: the coast is temperate and moderated by the Pacific Ocean; it can be arid in the south or in the shadows of the mountains, or have staggering amounts of rainfall; it can be freezing cold in the Arctic and on mountain slopes; and it can experience seasonal snowfall or scorching dry heat. The incredible heterogeneity of the landscape is mirrored in the vast range of ecological communities that occupy it.

The most notable ecological community is the Pacific Northwest rain forest. It is the largest temperate rain forest on earth and once stretched in an almost unbroken, majestic green swath from Alaska to California, bounded by the coast to the west and the mountains to the east. Today it is punctuated by regions that were clearcut for timber and development, and only about half of this incredible forest remains. Still, it is the epitome of a thriving, complex, and beautiful ecosystem and as iconic to the Northwest as is the salmon itself. Our image of a forest is dominated by trees, but all forests have a complex understory of shrubs and smaller plants, bushes, grasses, mosses, and ferns. There are epiphytic plants that grow on trunks and branches high in the forest canopy and a myriad of fungi and bacteria that cycle plant and animal debris in the soil. All forests are a critical resource. They regulate our climate, produce oxygen, store carbon, help filter groundwater, and prevent erosion during storms and floods.

As a rain forest implies, rainfall—in this case up to a phenomenal three meters of rain a year—is a critical environmental factor affecting its distribution and growth. The meteorology of the north Pacific ensures that moisture-laden air is transported from above the ocean to the coasts along the continent, and where it is pushed upward by the mountain ranges it cools and precipitation

condenses and drenches the land and forests below. This rain forest supports tens of thousands of species of plants and animals, including one of the largest and tallest organisms on earth, the coastal redwood, *Sequoia sempervirens*. Only the giant sequoia tree *(Sequoiadendron giganteum)* is more massive. Coastal redwoods can reach over 115 meters in height, have a volume exceeding 1,000 cubic meters of plant tissue, and live for over 1,000 years.

In the northern stretches of the temperate rain forest are the massive Sitka spruce *(Picea sitchensis)*, a giant growing up to eighty meters tall, and the western hemlock *(Tsuga heterophylla)*. And in the southern sections, coast Douglas-fir *(Pseudotsuga menziesii)*, western redcedar *(Thuja plicata)*, and shore pine *(Pinus contorta)* all stretch their branches high into the sky. Three of the

tallest tree species in the world are found in the Salmon Forest. There are also hardwood trees like the alder (*Alnus* sp.) and the bigleaf maple *(Acer macrophyllum)*, more common along stream and river banks and at lower elevations. These large forest canopy trees are excellent at catching moisture from drifting fog, and the drip from leaves and needles supplements the water from rain and snow, particularly during the dry summer months in the southern extensions of the forest into California. All these sources of precipitation help make the temperate rain forest extremely productive; it has a biomass higher than that of tropical rain forests like those in the Amazon basin. And the rain, melting snow, and fog drip collectively percolate through the soils and across the lush landscape and come together in the thousands of rushing streams and rivers in which the salmon swim.

○   ○   ○

THE FIRST MODERN FISHES, or at least those that fit our ichthy-
ological definition of convenience, appeared almost 400 million
years ago. The first primitive salmon appeared about 350 million years later, evidenced in the fossilized form of the beautiful-
ly named *Eosalmo driftwoodensis,* meaning "dawn salmon from
driftwood." The driftwood in this nomenclature refers to the name
of the creek in British Columbia that cuts through the shale and
sandstone beds where the fossil was first discovered, and not to
forest flotsam. In the millions of intervening years since the rise of
the modern fishes, our new salmon, *Eosalmo* sp., had evolved into
a form very similar to the Pacific salmon species that swim the rivers and oceans of today, with one major difference. The geologic
evidence from Driftwood Canyon and other fossil sites suggests
that the *Eosalmo* sp. that died and were so fortuitously and exqui-
sitely preserved in a fine rain of mud had lived in a landlocked lake
and did not migrate to the sea like their descendants, which now
divide their lives between the depths of the ocean and the shallow
streams of the Salmon Forest.

There are seven species of Pacific salmon and several trout that
live in the Salmon Forest. They are classified in the genus *Oncorhynchus,* which is a wonderful Latin moniker implying "hooked
snout," a reference to the fact that the first taxonomically described
specimens from western North America were adult males in their
transformed spawning guise. All organisms have a two-part name
as part of their biological classification. This taxonomic name, of
genus and species, provides both a unique classifier for identifica-
tion and description and a reference to each organism's evolutionary history. The most prominent Pacific salmon species' names
have a marvelous if convoluted pedigree, having been adopted

from the names given to the fish by the native Russian people of the Kamchatka Peninsula. These are sonorous words, thick with consonants: *gorbushcha, keta, kisutch, tshawytscha, mykiss,* and *nerka.* The local Koryak dialect names were phonetically documented by the famous German zoologist and explorer Georg Steller, who was one of the few survivors of Vitus Bering's ill-fated second expedition, which traveled through the Russian north Pacific and then ultimately, and tragically, to Alaska in 1741. These names were then incorporated into the first scientific description of these salmon species by the German physician-turned-taxonomist Johann Walbaum, who observed and collected them on his own exploratory journeys to the remote Kamchatka region almost fifty years later. And, because the modern Pacific salmon are not landlocked like the extinct *Eosalmo* sp., they have migrated around the entire north Pacific rim, as far south as Korea and California, and across Japan, Russia, Alaska, and the Canadian west coast.

What differentiates a salmon from other fish? Salmon taxonomy places them in the class Actinopterygii, or ray-finned fishes (having fins that are typically thin webs supported by bony spines), and order Salmoniformes, in which there are three salmonid subfamilies: the whitefishes, the graylings, and the salmon. In addition to some morphological features discernible only to a trained anatomist (like the shape and number of particular bones or the number of specific fin rays and scales), all salmon have a primitive adipose fin (a fatty, fin-shaped protuberance just anterior to the dorsal end of the tail), and although some spend part of their life cycle in the ocean, they all spawn in fresh or brackish water. There has been considerable debate over exact salmonid classification because of their great diversity, and even recently genus and species designations have changed as this commercially important group of fishes receives close scrutiny. The salmon subfamily includes the

chars and colloquially named trouts, as well as the fishes commonly known as the Atlantic and Pacific salmon. Here, by considering
those species critical to the landscape of the Pacific Northwest, we
concentrate on those fishes in the genus *Oncorhynchus*, but even
still, complexities in common and scientific naming persist. For
example, the now ubiquitous rainbow trout *Oncorhynchus mykiss*
and the cutthroat trout *O. clarki* were classified in the genus *Salmo* until modern genetic analysis confirmed their closer affinity to
Oncorhynchus and the Pacific salmon. And as we shall see, these
trouts possess an important life-history characteristic that keeps
them distinct from the Pacific salmon.

o   o   o

IF ANY of the Pacific salmon species were to be crowned king it
would be *Oncorhynchus tshawytscha*, the chinook. Judged by size
alone, chinook are majestic—mature chinook easily reach sixteen
kilograms, and behemoths of more than forty and even fifty kilograms are occasionally caught, making this the largest salmon
species. Chinook have been a critically important component of
Pacific Northwest society for as long as recorded history; First
Nation fisheries counted on the regular return of the chinook and
other salmon as a dominant food source. The first western settlers
on the Pacific coast of North America found a flourishing salmon fishery, and "chinook" is a reference to the name of the major tribe that inhabited the Columbia River basin. Today, annual
commercial catches may exceed 400,000 fish. These large fish favor the largest river drainages, which in the Pacific Northwest include the Columbia, Sacramento, and Yukon Rivers. Before modern societies' demand for electric power and the advent of hydro-
electric dams began to reshape the landscape, these mighty rivers

hosted spawning runs of millions of fish in one of the earth's most spectacular and lengthy migrations. To this day, chinook salmon still leave the Bering Sea and fight their way almost 3,000 kilometers upstream to breed in the headwaters of the still-virgin Yukon River.

The largest salmon also live the longest. In a process similar to tree ring dating, microscopic examination of seasonal ring patterns within their scales and otoliths (tiny lumps of calcium carbonate found in the salmon's inner ear and used to sense gravity) indicate that the magnificent chinook salmon, depending on the subpopulation, may reach sexual maturity after two years or may grow for up to nine years, swimming the ocean, before returning to their natal rivers and streams to spawn.

Although chinook lack some of the vibrant coloration of other salmon species, they are anything but drab. Chinook can have flesh that ranges in color from white to light pink to deep red; this is unusual for salmon, as most species show similar coloration throughout a population. Their scales and skin are a wonderful example of ocean-going cryptic coloration. Viewed from the side, they are a bright silver, which blends with the light blue and gray background of the sea. From the top, they appear a dark purplish blue to black, and from below, their bellies look white. This color scheme is advantageous to the seafaring chinook, whose succulent flesh is a prize for oceanic predators like sharks and a host of salmon-feeding marine mammals like orca, sea lions, and seals. A deep-swimming predator, attempting to discern the silhouette of an overhead salmon, may be unable to differentiate the white underbelly of the fish from the bright sunlit surface. A surface-swimming predator looking down—a sea lion, perhaps—will find it difficult to differentiate the dark-colored back of the chinook from the deep, dark water below. Both predators and prey adopt this camouflage. The same color patterning that helps the salmon evade those animals that want to eat it helps the salmon covertly hunt squid and the smaller fish like herring, pollack, and anchovy that make up its own seafaring diet. When chinook are fully mature and have begun their ultimate migration back to freshwater to spawn, their bodies turn a brown to dusky red color; presumably the cryptic coloring important in the ocean is not as important as adopting a coloration that signals a readiness to mate. And mature chinook, like all Pacific salmon, stop feeding once they begin their final swim back into the Salmon Forest.

In the language of the native Nanai people living along the Amur River in Sino-Russian Asia, the word *keta* implies simply "the fish." In their case, it refers specifically to large salmon, second in size to the chinook, which return yearly to spawn in streams tributary to the Amur and form a critical food source. *Keta* was appropriated as the species moniker for *Oncorhynchus keta* by the polymathic Johann Walbaum on his Asian travels. *Oncorhynchus keta* has the broadest geographic range of any salmon and swims the rivers and streams and seas from South Korea, around the north Pacific rim, all the way south to California and north to Canada's Yukon and Northwest Territory. In North America it is commonly known as the chum or dog salmon. When spawning, adults show dramatic coloration: vertical banding of red, purple, and black along their sides, and dark, olive-colored heads. In the language of the Chinook tribe, this is *tzum*, or "striped," becoming *chum* to the Anglo ear and pronunciation.

The other vernacular name for *Oncorhynchus keta*, dog salmon, is derivative of another spectacular morphological change that they, and other salmon to a greater or lesser degree, undergo when ready to spawn—their heads distend and grow enlarged dog-like canine teeth. Adult spawning salmon exhibit changes in body form that rival any metamorphosis in the animal kingdom. Beyond changes in coloration, heads enlarge, jaws extend and hook into what is referred to as a "kype," and backs may form a large, protruding hump between head and dorsal fin. Stomachs shrink, fins thicken, and skin absorbs scales and toughens in addition to changing coloration. All this metamorphosis requires fundamental changes in the salmon's physiology and anatomy, including the resorption and genesis of muscle, cartilage, and bone. These changes in morphology, often more enhanced in the males, can make the recently mature and the migratory spawning forms, or male and female sexes of the same fish, appear to be entirely different species, and in fact led to early taxonomic confusion. The spawning metamorphosis is important for completing the salmon life cycle; the new physical features are secondary sexual characteristics that signal egg-bearing females and may aid in the selection of mates. And although salmon do not feed while they are migrating upriver through the forest and spawning in the streams, the males fight each other for the chance to mate with nesting females. Then the fanged teeth and large hooked jaws, which are superfluous while starving, help determine the victors that will perpetuate the salmon population and pass on their genes—coded for bodies with the sharpest teeth and strongest jaws—to their offspring.

The most abundant salmon, *Oncorhynchus gorbuscha,* or pink salmon, is also the smallest. Adults typically weigh less than five kilograms, yet pink salmon comprise up to 40 percent of the world's commercial catch by weight and up to 60 percent of the catch by number. *Gorbuscha* in Russian means humpbacked, and the American nickname for these salmon is "humpies." This refers to the very large, prominent hump that forms in front of the dorsal fin of spawning males; the hump is present to a lesser degree

in females as well. Beneath their silvery-sided skin is archetypal pink-colored flesh, the "salmon pink" of our crayon boxes. These smaller fish are not as capable of fording fast-flowing water and negotiating waterfalls as the larger salmon species and as a consequence do not penetrate as deep into the coastal forests and landscape. In fact, pink salmon quite commonly use intertidal areas and estuaries for spawning. Pink salmon often gather in very large schools near their spawning streams, milling about before migrating en masse upstream in response to sudden changes in stream flow. And, unlike other salmon, individuals of *O. gorbuscha* typically live for about a year and a half to two years; three-year-old fish are rarely found. This particular life cycle results in the local formation of separate pink salmon populations that return to their natal streams in either even or odd years and rarely intermingle. Young pink and chum salmon spend very little time in freshwater and migrate almost directly to the sea soon after hatching, then disperse widely and may travel many thousands of kilometers in the north Pacific before returning to the coast.

The silver or coho salmon, *Oncorhynchus kisutch,* is a medium-sized salmon that is not as nomadic as the other species. Adults haunt the upper hundred meters or so of the continental shelf seas for two or three years before returning to short coastal streams to spawn. They are a subtly beautiful fish with backs of steely blue or black, sides of silver, and bellies of sparkling white. When spawning, *O. kisutch* flaunt pinkish bellies and sides that flush with red, green, and bronze hues. Unlike the pink and chum salmon, they have a more protracted relationship with freshwater ecosystems. The young spend two to three years in cold streams, rivers, and lakes before migrating to the ocean, and even then a precocious few take up only temporary residence in the sea—inhabiting estuaries in the spring and summer and returning to rivers and lakes in the fall and winter. They spawn later in the year than other species, the earliest migratory runs occurring in cold, steep mountain streams and the later runs, even as late as January, favoring migration into larger glacial rivers and deep lakes.

Oncorhynchus nerka were known to the native Chinook people as *sukkegh*, the "fish of fishes," which transformed in the Anglo vernacular into the common name sockeye. And it is the sockeye salmon that is now thought of as the quintessential fish of the Pacific Northwest. Its bright red, rich, fatty flesh has long been prized by both aboriginal and modern commercial fishermen. The sockeye embodies all the prodigious traits that Izaak Walton attributed to the king of fish. Sockeyes range across the north Pacific from the mountains and fjords of British Columbia to the sub-Arctic boreal forests of Russia's Kamchatka Peninsula. And though they are of

Packed tight together, migrating chum salmon *(Oncorhynchus keta)* battle their way upstream to spawning beds on Anan Creek, Alaska. ▼

moderate size, ten kilograms at the most, their tireless migratory spawning runs are among the longest of any salmon. Their feats of endurance are matched by their feats of strength; their ability to navigate raging mountain torrents and leap three- to five-meter waterfalls is legendary. Adult spawning sockeyes display an extraordinary and beautiful metamorphosis from their oceangoing form. Their white bellies, silver sides, and dark backs, similar to those of other salmon, transform for their migration. Males display vivid scarlet bodies, dark green heads, large humps, and exaggerated kypes. The females' spawning guise is only slightly more subdued than that of the males.

Like the pink salmon, sockeye amass in huge numbers and can be seen to choke river mouths, eddies, and pools as they migrate upstream, favoring rivers and streams that are connected with

lakes. The lakes are important for the life cycle of *O. nerka*. After hatching in the spring, the young move from spawning nests in connecting streams or on the lakeshore into the lake shallows, feeding on insects and aquatic larvae before moving into the deeper waters of the lake, where they feed almost exclusively on plankton. They spend two to three years in freshwater before migrating into the ocean, where they rapidly grow, again feeding predominantly on planktonic crustaceans, on squid, and occasionally on small fish. Sockeye spend an additional two to three years at sea, so adults that return to spawn are from four to six years in age.

One of the reasons that salmon are so successful is that they have been able to exploit the nutrient-rich waters of the north Pacific to feed and grow and then utilize the relative safety of coastal watersheds for reproduction. Sockeye exploit these principles further by using lakes as long-term nurseries and remaining planktivorous even in the ocean. Because of this, *O. nerka* provides us with a prime example of microevolution in action, in the form of the kokanee salmon, a landlocked variation of sockeye.

Not all sockeye salmon return to the ocean for their adult growth. The kokanee life cycle takes place entirely within freshwater, and natural populations can be found in landlocked lakes and rivers along the West Coast. This makes *Oncorhynchus nerka* unique among salmon species, which, if landlocked, never fully mature and die without being able to spawn. Kokanee flourish in deep lakes with a year-round planktonic food supply, and although they are typically smaller than the ocean-migrating sockeye, they are still fully capable of reproducing along gravelly lakeshores and lake-feeding rivers and streams. Sockeye and kokanee coexist in many of the same watersheds, and there are even locations where both forms spawn in the same streams and at the same time.

A sockeye salmon.

Microevolutionary processes force natural selection–driven changes on the genetic makeup within subpopulations of a species over a relatively short period of time, at least geologically. Charles Darwin first introduced the concept of natural selection, which has since become a critical framework upon which much of modern biology is formulated. Natural selection implies the differential survival of naturally varying individuals within a population. Some individuals naturally possess certain physical attributes that provide them with a reproductive advantage over others of the same species, and it is the genetic information, or genotype, coding for these advantageous characteristics, like extra-powerful jaws or swimming muscle endurance, that is passed on to the next generation. These selective processes are one of the mechanisms by which new species—in this case, of salmon—are created. Microevolutionary processes act upon the genotype of a single population of a species, whereas macroevolutionary processes tend to operate over longer periods of time, the compounded effects of many microevolutionary steps acting on different species as a whole. These processes are ultimately what creates both sockeye and kokanee, as well as what makes *O. nerka* different from *O. gorbuscha* and *O. mykiss*, and salmon different from swordfish, and the fish of the Pacific Northwest different from trees along the shore.

New species are formed by the very slow and gradual buildup of genetic differences from one form to another, until ultimately there are enough differences between them that they can no longer interbreed and reproduce; this is the process of anagenesis. Another microevolutionary process, cladogenesis, is slightly different; there is an evolutionary splitting event, a divergence that ultimately creates a new species from the ancestor. The splitting event that leads to the divergence could be any number of things that causes separate populations of a single species to become reproductively isolated. In the case of *O. nerka* and the kokanee, it could be the natural blockage of a spawning river or the isolation of a nursery lake. Because *O. nerka* can survive, and most critically, reproduce when confined to a freshwater habitat, they continue to grow and spawn and populate their restricted watershed. This new habitat poses different environmental challenges than does a life cycle in which juveniles and adults live in the sea, and so there is a subtle accumulation of changes, guided by natural selection, in the isolated population, which begins to diverge from the original ocean-migrating sockeye. In the case of the kokanee, this has resulted in an obvious difference in body size; even when fully mature, kokanee are smaller than sockeye, which limits interbreeding between them. It has also resulted in a number of differences only noticeable at the genetic level—like variations in coding sequences in specific regions of mitochondrial DNA—that are nonetheless distinctive. What is even more fascinating is that this kind of cladogenesis, the creation of kokanee from landlocked sockeye, has happened more than once, in lakes and watersheds that are geographically very widely separated, and these differences are still reflected in subtle yet measurable variations in the genes of sockeye and kokanee.

Kokanee *(Oncorhynchus nerka)* school along the shore of Lake Tahoe, more than 300 kilometers from the ocean. Generations of reproductive isolation have led the smaller kokanee to evolve from the original sockeye salmon species.

But kokanee and sockeye are still the same species because, despite their differences, they still occasionally interbreed and produce viable offspring. Interbreeding in this case is often by the actions of "sneaks," small kokanee males that stealthily spawn with nesting sockeye females while the sockeye males are occupied elsewhere, fighting for dominance. The hybrid progeny of sockeye-kokanee mating are not as fit as offspring from "pure" sockeye or kokanee pairings, in both a physical and an evolutionary sense. The hybrids show a reduced capacity for tolerating changes in salinity, lower swimming performance, and slower developmental growth. They survive but are presumably not as competitive against their purebred cousins, which are better adapted to the selective pressures of a life lived strictly in a freshwater lake or a life that migrates to and from the ocean. If the hybrids were as successful, they would be constantly diluting the local *O. nerka* gene pool and the kokanee wouldn't be diverging from the sockeye in form and behavior. Given enough time, if the kokanee and sockeye remain isolated they may give rise to separate species as the Salmon Forest continues to evolve.

There are two other Pacific salmon that populate the seas and coastal landscapes from Korea to Russia and never crossed the

Bering Sea. *Oncorhynchus rhodurus* is a small fish and, like the sockeye-kokanee, can be found in two types, a landlocked *biwa-masu* form and a stream-dwelling, seagoing *amago* type. The other Asian salmon, *Oncorhynchus masou*, is very similar in appearance to the silver salmon of the Pacific Northwest and is closely related to *O. rhodurus*. Their similarity is so great that the taxonomic separation of the species has been debated; some ichthyologists consider them the same species, making their plastic and evolving life history and ecology remarkably similar to that of the North American sockeye and kokanee. Considered as distinct species, *O. masou*, like *O. rhodurus*, has populations that live strictly in freshwater and populations that migrate to the ocean and return to freshwater to spawn. They are commonly known as *masu* or *yamame* (the ocean form), which has a delightful symbolic kanji translation as "mountain woman fish." On the islands of Japan, the vernacular for *O. masou* is *sakura masu*, the cherry salmon, because the adults return to spawn in the rivers and streams when the cherry trees begin to blossom. There is also a deeper, more aesthetic link to *sakura* that the salmon embodies. The eighteenth-century Buddhist scholar Motoori Norinaga developed the concept of *mono no aware*, which would become a crucial philosophy defining Japanese culture. Quite literally it is the "pathos of things," empathy with the natural world and its transient state and compassion for life. The ephemeral quality of the beautiful cherry blossoms, like the mass spawning and subsequent death of the salmon in the streams among the trees, becomes a metaphor for the delicate and fleeting nature of life and its rebirth.

The present salmon populations in the Pacific Northwest stem from relict populations that have been extant since the last ice age, the Tioga advance of the Wisconsinan glacial episode, which ended approximately 15,000 years ago. Prior to that, the Laurentide ice sheet covered most of the present range of *Oncorhynchus* with the exception of two areas: Cascadia, which was in the region of the lower Columbia River valley, and Beringia, which was located in the northwest through the central-north Pacific and included the land bridge from Alaska to Siberia. These two ice-free regions served as refuges for freshwater and ocean-running fish for the entire region, as reflected in mitochondrial DNA from *O. nerka* collected all across the Pacific. Sockeye and kokanee collected from northern British Columbia, western Alaska, and Kamchatka are closely related, and there is a southern group from the Columbia and Fraser River systems with historical connections to Cascadia. The distribution and genetic makeup of the salmon that we have today are a result of the two refuge populations straying into recently ice-free and unoccupied habitat and then being shaped by the prevalent forces of microevolution. This very dynamic process involves geographic isolation, adaptation to the local environment, genetic divergence, and competition among interacting populations. This means that across the vast extent of the Salmon Forest there are now many hundreds of genetically distinct populations of each salmon species, with each population in genetic balance between processes that reinforce further isolation and processes that mix them back together.

We would be remiss if we did not at least mention the five species of Atlantic salmon, genus *Salmo,* of which there is only one true salmon, *Salmo salar,* Walton's crowned fish monarch, with a distribution that spans from the Gulf of Saint Lawrence through Scandinavia and the British Isles to northern Spain. The other four Atlantic species are all freshwater trouts, sport fish common around the world. It is thought that *Salmo* and *Oncorhynchus* shared a common ancestor about twenty million years ago, a conclusion based on genetic molecular clock techniques that examine the sequence structure of amino acids in certain growth hormone genes common to both fish groups. Fossil evidence suggests that most of the differences between *Salmo* and *Oncorhynchus* evolved over the next fifteen million years or so, centered in what was to become the Pacific Northwest, before the beginning of the Pliocene epoch. The ancestral fishes populated the drainages of the ancient continent of Laurasia (which would become North America, Greenland, Europe, and Asia), and fossils of many different salmon species can be found in rock strata between six and seven million years old in what is now Oregon and Idaho (including fossils of a spectacular extinct three-meter-long "sabertooth salmon," *Oncorhynchus rastrosus*).

The north Atlantic Ocean began to form about fifty-five million years ago, when the continental plates Laurentia and Eurasia began to tear apart. The Pacific Ocean has a more primitive origin; it is the remnant of the Panthalassic Ocean, which surrounded the ancient supercontinent of Pangea until about 170 million years ago. At the time of the formation of the Atlantic, the two oceans remained separated by land—there was no Arctic Ocean linkage. Then about four million years ago an oceanic connection occurred, as evinced by the sudden appearance of Pacific benthic fossils (like clams) in the rock history of Iceland. *Oncorhynchus* and *Salmo* were geographic contemporaries until relatively recently in a geologic time frame, evolving in step with the ancient landscape they inhabited. Now the two genera are isolated, their progeny continuing to evolve but restricted to the drainages of the north Pacific *(Oncorhynchus)* or Atlantic *(Salmo)* because the present central Arctic Ocean climate provides a barrier as impassable as the land bridge between continents was millions of years ago. Whether this remains the case as the earth's climate alters is another story.

LIFE AND DEATH OF A SALMON

HERE ARE some remarkable traits common to all Pacific salmon regardless of taxonomic etymology and the numerous variations in each species' coloration, size, or shape of mouth. They all live in the northern hemisphere and have adipose fins, small smooth-edged scales, forward-stretching gill tissues, and peculiarities in vertebra shape, but the most important commonality that explains much of the essence of the Salmon Forest and separates them from their trout brethren is that the salmon in genus *Oncorhynchus* are *semelparous*. Taken from the Latin, *semelparous* means "begotten once," a reference to their lyrical existence: they die soon after they reproduce. This one characteristic separates them from all the closely related trout and the Atlantic *Salmo salar*. And because these spawning salmon return to the streams whence they were born, they fulfill their poetic life to the utmost: their birthplace, and that of their offspring, becomes their grave.

What may seem to be a counterintuitive life strategy, to "live fast and die young" just as they reach their reproductive potential, is a finely tuned and effective evolutionary strategy that, above all other things, seeks to maximize the transfer of genetic material from one generation to the next. Life as a maturing salmon is rife with hazards and mortality is very high during a lifetime of migration from a freshwater mountain stream to the open ocean and then back again. It is astonishing that any reproductively viable adults return to spawn at all considering the gauntlet of predators, from fishes to fishermen, and the host of environmental challenges, from blocked or silted river beds to radical changes in temperature and salinity, that salmon must navigate. In a final effort to maximize their reproductive potential, adult Pacific salmon expend all their energy during their upstream spawning run and the final acts of reproduction itself. Males fight and compete for mates until scarred and emaciated, and females invest their last metabolic energy in egg production and in guarding their nests until they become too weak and battered to hold their position in the current, and then they drift away to die.

○   ○   ○

SALMON LIFE, like much in the animal kingdom, begins with an egg. Salmon are oviparous, which means that females lay their eggs and the embryos develop and hatch outside the female's body. Salmon eggs are among the largest of all the bony fish eggs and a magnificent example of practical and aesthetic beauty. They are exquisite golden orange and red spheres, just less than a centimeter across, holding a nucleus of maternal genetic material and packed full of nutritious yolk. They are surrounded by a tough yet porous membrane that is strong enough to withstand the rigors of being buried in gravel and sand at the bottom of a rushing stream, yet permeable enough to allow oxygen to enter and carbon dioxide and other wastes to be flushed from the egg as the embryo develops.

A female salmon produces these large nutritious eggs at great metabolic expense, particularly because salmon do not feed during their final spawning migration. In essence, she sacrifices herself in order to produce offspring that have the highest chance of survival because they develop with their own integrated food reserve—the large yolk. At the same time, the salmon must strike an evolutionary balance between the size of an individual egg and the number of eggs she can produce. Large eggs enhance the early survival of offspring, but being more fecund increases the number of offspring in the nest as they begin a life that has a high chance of early mortality, and so salmon typically lay a few thousand eggs in a nest (although a large chinook can lay more than fifteen thousand eggs). A large yolk can provide enough energy for an embryo and then a newly hatched young still attached to the yolk sac (an "alevin") to survive a fall spawn through the winter. But the large nutrient-filled yolk also makes the eggs (as well as egg-laden females) a preferred food for a host of forest predators. Indeed, when streams are flush with spawning salmon and the fishing is relatively easy, salmon-feeding bears are known to strip and eat only the egg-filled gonad and leave the rest of the salmon carcass on the forest floor or stream bank. Female salmon expend energy not just producing their eggs but investing in parental care. The act of locating a suitable spot and digging a nest, or "redd," by beating the bottom with her sides and tail to form a clean depression, and then burying the eggs further once fertilized by a suitor's milt, increases the odds that her offspring will survive, but it is ultimately costly to the mother. Although spent from these acts, she guards the nest until all her energy reserves are consumed, then leaves behind orphans with the best achievable chance of hatching.

Because the eggs are incubated under a layer of sediment for protection, optimal nesting areas are in streams and rivers with well-aerated waters and beds of clean, well-sorted gravel and sand. The exact timing of embryonic development and hatching, like much of the salmon's life history, varies among species and even

among subpopulations of the same species, because it is closely adapted to the particular local environment that each population inhabits. Development is a function of water temperature (with slower development in colder waters) and the amount of dissolved oxygen present (with slower development in waters with lower oxygen levels). Populations living in the coldest northern waters, and that spawn late in the year, inherently develop slowly, and hatching and further development then occur in the spring, when temperatures increase and more food is available. Mortality is very high in the nest, approaching 90 percent in some species, because the eggs and hatchlings are at the mercy of a profusion of physical challenges besides the risk of being eaten. They are susceptible to reduced oxygen levels from siltation, to unfavorable displacement, and to damage and death from scouring of the bottom. After hatching, the alevins, which are still attached to their yolk sacs, are physically incapable of swimming against any current, so their first behavior is to push downward, away from light and further into the gravel, and then gravitate toward water flow and higher oxygen levels as they slowly disperse. For the most part, they remain inactive and survive off the nutrients provided by their yolk, which feeds the development of their internal organ systems as it is metabolized. Once the yolk is fully consumed, the alevin,

◄ *(Top)* Salmon eggs are glistening orange-red spheres whose yolks are packed with nutrients to feed the growing embryo. Their beauty is matched by their robust utility; the eggs are tough enough to withstand burial in stream sediments but also allow oxygen and waste products to diffuse across their outer skin. The dark spots are the rapidly developing eyes of the young larvae.

◄ *(Bottom)* Recently hatched larvae, or alevin, still attached to their yolk sacs. The yolk provides the nutrients for alevin growth and development even through the winter months; however, its high caloric content makes the alevin a prime target for predation.

now known as "fry," typically wriggle up through the gravel and emerge into the overlying water at night to begin their residence in streams and small rivers, or in the case of some, like the sockeye, in the shallows of adjoining lakes.

Salmon fry, and the larger juvenile stage, "parr," continue to slowly develop and grow in the freshwaters of the forest, and in order to survive must balance their own need to feed on insects, insect larvae, and plankton with the task of avoiding being eaten themselves. They are at risk even from other salmon. Some species, like the pink salmon, seek almost immediately to swim to the ocean, where planktonic food is much more abundant and growth is accelerated, but which is also populated by a much larger number of predators. Juveniles take advantage of whatever habitat is available to maximize feeding and avoid predators. They will shift between habitats seasonally and from day to night, hiding under river banks during the day and moving into more open water in the evening. In fact it is the quantity and quality of the salmon-friendly habitable spaces in a stream that ultimately determine the number and size of developing salmon that it can support. Because the lakes, rivers, and streams are intrinsically variable in the Pacific Northwest due to seasonal changes in flow, local rainfall patterns, and the wooded terrain, the landscape we refer to as the Salmon Forest reveals itself as an optimal environment for salmon. A local flooding event, a debris flow that alters watershed drainage, or even a fallen tree that partially blocks a stream may appear catastrophic in the short run, but in the long term these events create a diversity of microhabitats that can accommodate many different life stages and even different species of salmon all in one region.

Towering old-growth forest on the Olympic Peninsula, Washington State. ▶

The plankton-rich waters of the north Pacific Ocean can provide much more food to a growing salmon than can a freshwater river or stream, and the high metabolic rates of developing salmon can sustain rapid growth as long as food is available. Rapid growth is critical because survival in the ocean is generally size selective— small fish get eaten—so salmon must either enter the ocean at a large size or grow rapidly once they enter salt water. Each spring, salmon populations face the challenge of whether or not they should migrate from their freshwater havens to the ocean bounty. As we know from the kokanee, some select not to migrate at all. Larger juveniles in good health tend to migrate downstream to the sea, while smaller ones are more likely to persist in their freshwater habitats for another year. The evolutionary need for migration is prompted by parr size and the internal physiological rhythms of development and is linked to environmental cues such as increases in temperature and day length. A salmon parr that is undergoing the behavioral, developmental, and physical transition from freshwater to salt water is known as a "smolt."

The Pacific salmon life that has evolved to include development stages initiating in freshwater, maturity in the ocean, and then the critical return to freshwater to spawn is called an *anadromous* life history, and smolting is essential to it. Anadromy (from the Greek meaning "up running") is another common trait of salmon and some trouts that differentiates them from other members of Salmonidae. For instance, the steelhead form of rainbow trout, *O. mykiss,* is an anadromous trout that spends two or three years at sea and returns to freshwater to spawn (however, it is not semelparous and can spawn up to four times, so it is not referred to as a salmon). The converse life history, known as *catadromy,* wherein a life spent predominantly in freshwater is punctuated by the requirement to migrate and spawn in the ocean, is also found in

fishes. *Anguilla anguilla* and *A. rostrata*, the freshwater eels of Europe and America, are the most famous catadromous fishes, migrating thousands of kilometers from rivers and lakes to spawn in the Sargasso Sea in the mid-Atlantic.

Anadromy and the requirement that a salmon be adapted to live in both fresh- and salt water necessitate a physiological miracle. To explain this, we need to develop a new analogy for our salmon archetype. I suggest that of a leaky boat—even though a leaky boat might seem to be the antithesis of everything that equates with being a fish.

It is a testament to evolution, ours and the salmon's, that each cell in the body of a human or fish or bear in the forest contains vital fluid—cytoplasm—that closely mimics the composition of seawater. Each cell is a finely tuned machine of its own, adapted to a life in seawater in our ancestors eons ago. Even after innumerable generations and adaptations for survival as a single entity or as one small part of an organ system in the complex mechanism that is a salmon, a cell's internal components only function properly when they are bathed in a cytoplasm with the correct concentration of salts and ions. And water itself is essential for the physiological and biochemical functioning of every organism on earth. If a fish were perfectly sealed, it might be able to maintain the correct internal chemistry regardless of where it lived, but it is not. It is a leaky boat because a fish contains millions of semipermeable membranes that are exposed to the environment, and it must eat and breathe and excrete, and doing so changes the chemistry of its body fluids. A tuna placed in a lake or a goldfish placed in the sea quickly dies because an imbalance in internal chemistry leads to a failure at the cellular level, which cascades to a failure of the whole. A fish's gills are its leakiest organ. The tissues there are thin, folded, and extend into long filaments, adaptations that maximize surface area in order to absorb oxygen most efficiently from the water flushing over the gills and pass that oxygen into the bloodstream. While very effective for respiration, this design allows other molecules, both beneficial and detrimental, to enter and leave the body. A fish must breathe, yet the gills act like a gaping hole in the bottom of a boat, with water wanting to rush either in or out, depending on whether the boat is sitting in the sea or drifting down a river. Life in a stream and life in the ocean are physiologically very different, yet a salmon manages to stabilize the ionic chemistry of its internal fluids and can therefore live in both.

The process that governs the movement of molecules between solutions and through permeable membranes, like those in cell walls and salmon gills, is osmosis. It is actually a result of the essential thermodynamic principle of entropy—a statistical measure of the degree of randomness in the world. Molecules will move about fluids and through permeable membranes so that the entropy of the total system is maximized. In cells and salmon this means that water molecules tend to move automatically through permeable membranes from regions that have a low concentration of dissolved ions into areas that have a higher concentration of dissolved ions. Osmosis controls many passive biochemical processes in all living things because life tends to be assembled of inordinate numbers of tiny fluid-filled compartments (tissues and cells and the microscopic organelles within cells), each filled with various dissolved ions and molecules, all separated by membranes. If a cell is placed into a solution that has a higher concentration of dissolved ions, water escapes the cell and it will wither and collapse. If it is kept in a solution with a lower concentration of ions, water will rush into the cell and it will expand and eventually burst. Most simply, any fish in a river tends to swell because water molecules osmotically flow into the fish's tissues, where the ions are maintained at a higher concentration relative to the freshwater. In the ocean the opposite is true: water flows out of the fish's body because the concentration of dissolved ions is lower there than in the sea.

In this discussion of the leaky salmon we are most interested in the balance of sodium and chloride ions—that is, the "salt" in seawater—that surrounds the fish, and the constituents of the body fluids, like the blood and the cell cytoplasm. Cells require the correct concentration of many different dissolved ions and molecules,

which includes dissolved nutrients as well as salts, and complex osmoregulatory mechanisms have evolved in order to maintain a delicate balance of stable internal osmotic conditions. For a fish this means maintaining relatively high levels of sodium and chloride ions and low levels of other ions like potassium, calcium, and magnesium. Osmoregulation—controlling the internal ionic chemistry—requires metabolic energy, not just to conserve ion balance and the correct volume of water, but also to aid the transport of toxic organic and inorganic waste molecules out of cells, where they are produced as a result of constant cellular metabolism. This metabolism is the life-sustaining series of chemical reactions that occur in all living beings either to consume energy in order to assemble new molecules, like proteins, or to break down larger molecules in order to release energy that can be used for other processes, like those necessary for maintaining ionic balance. Osmosis itself is passive and is exploited by the cell to aid in the transport of substances across cellular membranes. Osmotic flow, or pressure, is developed across membranes where a gradient exists between low and high concentrations of ions, and for the case of sodium and potassium ions, these gradients are exploited as a potential energy source for trans-membrane transport. But maintaining the ionic gradients requires the actions of special structures—microscopic protein pumps—that span cell membranes and that can shuttle ions against osmotic gradients as long as there is metabolic energy available to power them.

Details aside, it is paramount for a salmon, or any fish, or any animal for that matter, to maintain the correct composition of its internal fluids, because that composition is critical for cellular function and hence life. Osmoregulatory mechanisms exist at the level of individual cells, as well as in tissues and organs that have evolved to actively filter or compartmentalize fluids that are waste filled or in osmotic disequilibrium and then transport them away from cells and out of the body. Salmon are special because they can perform this critical osmoregulation in either freshwater or salt water.

In freshwater, a salmon is a leaky boat that is continuously flooding with water, and to continue the nautical analogy, the salmon's kidneys must then perform as extremely efficient bilge pumps to help maintain the osmotic balance of the body. The kidney functions to remove the excess water absorbed into the bloodstream and then excretes it as a very dilute urine. Because a salmon in freshwater is swimming in a medium that is more dilute, with fewer salts, than are in its internal body fluids and cells, it constantly loses critical ions back into the environment. So a freshwater-adapted kidney is designed with glomerulii and renal tubules (specialized tissues forming the internal filtering apparatus of the kidney) that are very efficient at resorbing crucial salts and electrolytes back into the bloodstream. The process isn't 100 percent effective and important ions are always lost, so the salmon must replace them by other means. Some are replaced during the ingestion of food, and critical salts are absorbed through the intestine. But more important, critical ions like sodium and chloride are actively transported, against osmotic gradients from the surrounding water, into the blood by special cells in the gills. The huge surface area of the gill makes it an osmotic liability, yet is vitally important for oxygen intake and is packed with specialized chloride cells that have deeply folded or "invaginated" membranes and are full of mitochondria (the microscopic "power engines" within cells) and important enzymes. By consuming metabolic energy, the chloride cells actively absorb key ions from the environment and maintain the supply of crucial ions to the body.

As a smolt swims downstream into salt water, the osmotic forces are effectively reversed. In fact, from an osmoregulatory standpoint, a life in seawater is much more challenging than one in freshwater, because the osmotic gradient between a salmon and the ocean is much larger than that between a salmon and a stream. The leaky boat now loses water into the surrounding sea. The salmon replaces the lost water by actively gulping seawater that is absorbed by the intestine. But the intestine cannot absorb water without also absorbing the ocean's salts into the bloodstream. To retain the ionic balance, the kidney now must function to filter and retain water, and in the gill, the chloride cells and their internal structure reorganize to excrete sodium and chloride ions out of the bloodstream and back into the ocean. What of a sailor lost at sea—Coleridge's drifting mariners, perhaps? Unlike ocean-adapted salmon, human sailors cannot survive drinking seawater because our kidneys can't produce a urine sufficiently concentrated to preserve our body's delicate ionic balance and conserve water while eliminating all the excess salt ingested with the seawater.

The physiological processes involved during smolting are under the developmental control of a complicated mix of hormones. This hormone bath is secreted by the salmon's thyroid, pituitary, and interrenal glands, which themselves receive environmental and developmental cues to regulate the timing of the physiological and cellular transformations. The changes required to adapt fully to a life in the sea take some time before they are fully functional; some shifts in cellular ion pumping can occur in less than a day, while other more complex tissue adaptations take longer. Salmon smolts are fortunately very tolerant of shifts in ionic and osmotic balance and can survive the transition to salt water while their bodies are still transforming from a former life in streams and rivers.

With its physiology and anatomy at least partially prepared for a life in salt water, a smolt leaves the rivers of the coastal watershed for the sea. Intermediate between rivers and the open sea are the estuaries at river mouths along the coast, and these serve as transitional stops for salmon en route to the ocean. Estuaries have complex physical environments driven by interactions between river flows and ocean tides. Water depth, temperature, current speeds and directions, turbidity and salinity, and food sources all vary over small distances and on time scales varying from tidal to seasonal cycles. The growth of salmon is rapid in estuaries, and the wide diversity of habitats allows these coastal zones to be exploited to different extents by different salmon species; they feed, changing their diet as they grow, and may use the brackish water found in parts of an estuary to ease the physiological transition of smolting. Some species remain longer than others and linger in estuaries, fjords, or near shore before heading into the open ocean, usually by late summer, and then don't return to the Salmon Forest until they are fully mature and ready to spawn.

In the open sea, salmon life is enigmatic. This is true for most pelagic fishes because of the extreme difficulty of studying creatures that roam vast areas of the planet. Our only glimpse of their peripatetic lives comes from the brief hint of their ecology we can deduce when they are caught. There is some evidence that their patterns of dispersal have some genetic basis: sockeye, pink, and chum salmon tend to favor the open ocean, while chinook and coho salmon are often found in coastal areas. And oceanic conditions undoubtedly affect their ranging and life at sea, for despite its overwhelming size, the ocean does not provide a uniform environment from season to season and year to year. In the Pacific, the El Niño / Southern Oscillation (ENSO), which is the periodic variation in ocean surface temperature and climate, causes changes in the thermal structure of the sea and alters coastal current flow and the strength of upwelling current features along the coast of the Americas. These changes then affect the biology and distribution not just of salmon but of the organisms that the salmon feed on. When surface temperatures warm and the amount of nutrient-rich upwelling waters decreases (during an El Niño), warm-water tropical species move northward and colder-water species, like the salmon, must forage farther north or into deeper, cooler waters. The changes in their environment can cause reduced growth and increase the chance of mortality because growth is coupled with prey availability and temperature.

o   o   o

SALMON HAVE evolved to leave the freshwater terrestrial ecosystems where they are born and then to feed and rapidly grow in the rich waters of the north Pacific. They are one of the most numerous of the fishes that swim the upper waters of the seas and thus are a critical component in the north Pacific Ocean ecosystem; by their numbers alone they affect an incredible diversity of organisms either as a competitor for resources, a predator, or prey. Because survival in the ocean is very size selective, the majority of salmon that manage to survive the perils of development in a streambed nest, through smolting, do not to manage to return to the forest. Small creatures survive either by existing in vast numbers and reproducing quickly (like many zooplankton and phytoplankton) or by growing very rapidly beyond the size that makes them an easy one-gulp meal. In the ocean arena, where the size of an animal's gape and the ferocity of its feeding bite often determine what eats what, salmon are opportunistic hunters and feed on a diet of zooplankton, krill, small fishes (even other salmon), and small crustaceans when they are immature and then move to larger fishes and squid as they continue to grow. Similarly, salmon are preyed upon by an abundance of predators like seabirds, dogfish, and other larger salmon when they are small, and when larger become the preferred prey of seals, sea lions, sharks, orca, and humans.

A salmon must continuously traverse a gauntlet of predators that includes some of the largest and fiercest of the ocean's inhabitants. Among the largest, humpback whales *(Megaptera novaeangliae)* are important seasonal visitors to north Pacific pelagic and coastal waters. Curiously, despite their enormous size they feed on the smaller salmon. It is estimated that up to 20,000 humpbacks migrate into the region to feed in the nutrient-rich waters during the summer months and then migrate south into tropical waters to mate and calve during the winter. Different subpopulations of humpback whales migrate from these feeding grounds to breeding sites off Mexico and the Hawaiian Islands, and southeast of Japan. Like the other great baleen whales that frequent the northern waters to feed, such as the sei *(Balaenoptera borealis),* the fin *(Balaenoptera physalus),* and the much smaller minke *(Balaenoptera acutorostrata),* they feed primarily on krill and small schooling fishes like herring, pilchard, mackerel, and small salmon. Although not always preying on the salmon directly, they are important to the salmon's life-history cycle because they also feed on fishes that compete directly with the salmon for food. Their sieve-like feeding anatomy, their baleen-stuffed mouths, which gives this group of whales its name, is optimized for separating small prey items from the huge gulps of water the whales capture in their mouths and expandable throats. After a gulp, they squeeze out the water, past the baleen plates that separate and concentrate the krill and small fishes for ingestion.

Humpback whales that winter in Alaska and British Columbia are unique in their use of cooperative bubble-net feeding techniques. In a spectacular display of organized feeding, groups of

The pelagic crab *(Pleuroncodes planipes)*, which extends its range into the Northern California current during El Niño periods, is just one of a multitude of planktonic creatures that are part of the salmon's north Pacific food web.

Beautiful Pacific white-sided dolphins *(Lagenorhynchus obliquidens)* roam deeper waters off the Pacific continental shelves from Mexico to Alaska. They are a small part of a gauntlet of predators that feed on maturing salmon in the open seas.

Harbor seal *(Phoca vitulina)* resting on an ice floe in Misty Fjord, Alaska. Salmon form an important part of the seasonal diet of north Pacific seals and sea lions. Unfortunately, competition between these animals and people for increasingly scarce salmon resources has led to the euthanization of seals and sea lions, which are considered a nuisance to fishing stocks.

whales encircle schools of prey in a ring of exhaled bubbles that serves to concentrate the fish in a small area, maximizing feeding efficiency for the entire group. The whole event is extremely well choreographed. Deep-diving individuals locate the prey school and begin to envelop it in a curtain of air bubbles expelled from their blowholes. Other whales use loud vocalizations to herd errant prey into the rising bubble net. By carefully spiraling upward and continuing to exhale, the whales drive the school of prey fish toward the surface and into an ever-tightening ball. Then, on cue, the whales surface through the center of the bubble net, mouths agape, capturing hundreds or thousands of fish in titanic gulps.

Among the fiercest of the oceanic marine predators, orca *(Orcinus orca)*, like salmon, are iconic animals of the Pacific Northwest. Adult orca are apex predators in oceanic ecosystems, with no predators of their own, and they are the largest of the Delphinidae (dolphins). They are toothed whales with distinctive black and white coloration, large dorsal fins, and powerful bodies that can attain about ten meters in length. Some orca live in complex matriarchal societies, although all tend to form pods of at least a few related individuals and engage in sophisticated cooperative behavior.

There are three separate races of orca from Washington State through Canada, Alaska, and the Aleutian Islands, and these differ in distribution, behavior, and social structure. The "offshore" race seldom approaches the shore and is believed to feed primarily on schooling fish, like the salmon, and occasionally other marine mammals and sharks. The other two races have overlapping

◄ Humpback whales *(Megaptera novaeangliae)* are influential seasonal visitors to the north Pacific. They feed primarily on krill and small schooling fishes, including immature salmon. Even when not preying on salmon directly, humpbacks are linked to them trophically because they feed on fishes that compete with salmon for food.

ranges along the coast but seldom interact or collocate. The "transient" orca race forms small pods of less than ten individuals and feeds almost exclusively on other marine mammals and birds, including sea lions, seals, porpoise, small baleen whales, and other dolphins. Although they can echolocate and have an extensive vocal repertoire, they remain relatively quiet when hunting, presumably to avoid alerting their prey.

The third orca race, "residents," has a more complex pod social structure and feeds primarily on fish. Resident pods tend to follow salmon in their spawning migration, and even though they are known to prey on about two dozen different fish species, salmon make up over 95 percent of their diet. They feed primarily on chinook and coho, presumably because they are the largest and have the highest lipid content of the salmon species, and they continue to target chinook and coho even when those species are present in low numbers and other salmon are locally more abundant. A single orca can consume more than 200 kilograms of salmon a day. When captured, large salmon are sometimes carried to the surface and torn apart for sharing with other pod members. Fish-hunting orca use high-intensity echolocating clicks to localize their prey from as far as 100 meters away, and it is possible that the returning sound pulses provide enough information to the whales to allow them to discriminate different fish species. Experiments on the

Some pods of humpback whales use cooperative bubble-net feeding techniques when hunting fish, surrounding their prey with a ring of bubbles from their blowholes. The rising bubble ring concentrates the prey, which are then swallowed from below as the whales rush toward the surface.

sensory physiology of salmon have shown that they are incapable of detecting sound frequencies higher than about 400 hertz. The echolocating clicks generated by the orca produce most of their energy in frequencies between 45 and 80 kilohertz, a frequency at least 100 times higher, which would be undetectable to salmon prey.

It is only recently, in a geologic time sense, that a more fearsome salmon predator has arrived in the Salmon Forest and north Pacific—humans. Our predatory capabilities have rapidly evolved from the first native fishermen who stalked the banks of salmon streams with nets and spears. Now our nets have mouths that gape much farther than the mouths of the largest baleen whales, our longlines have hooks for teeth and form jaws that stretch for kilometers, and our fishing ships range tirelessly along the coast and into the roughest of seas and are equipped with echolocating sensors that rival those of the orca. Very quickly we have become the most important salmon predator and the apex predator for the entire world.

Survival isn't merely a question of eating or being eaten; salmon have intricate ecological relationships that affect their chances of ever reaching reproductive maturity. They compete with other fishes like herring and hake for similar prey, and the degree of competition depends on their age and size and the availability of the food resource, which varies in time and space. And salmon succumb to a host of different parasites and pathogens. As it is for most creatures on earth, life as a salmon is difficult, and living long enough to procreate can seem nothing short of a miracle.

The saying goes that "the star that burns twice as bright burns half as long," and a salmon burns very, very bright. Their high metabolic rate allows salmon to grow rapidly as long as food is available, and they obtain more than 95 percent of their body mass while at sea. But they sacrifice longevity for their rapid growth rate, and therefore become fully mature quite quickly. The more northerly salmon tend to be slightly older when mature—a chinook salmon in the cold Bering Sea may be as old as nine. However, most salmon are fully mature in two to five years, depending on the species, which is not a long period considering that much of that time may be spent in freshwater prior to smolting. Assuming that a salmon can survive until it is sexually mature, it then responds to a mix of inherent developmental cues and environmental signals and begins another epic migration; it stops roaming the ocean and returns to its natal stream, sometimes traveling thousands of kilometers.

Returning to its natal stream is a daunting challenge for a fish that can range so widely. Again the salmon must manage a transition in environments, from the relatively stable conditions of the open ocean to the much more complex physical environment of the coastal zone, with its bays, reefs, islands, strong and reversible tidal currents, fluctuating temperatures, and changing salinity. But first, a salmon must navigate back to the coast, and to the correct river mouth location, and at precisely the right time to meet and run upstream with its cohort.

The exact means by which salmon can navigate so accurately while in the open ocean are not well understood. They don't wander randomly through the varying oceanic conditions; instead, they migrate on a relatively straight course toward their birthplace. This implies that they have some type of internal map and compass capability that allows them to navigate as well as to be temporally and geospatially aware. Juvenile and larval salmon are sensitive to the overhead position of the sun as well as to patterns of polarization in the sky, and although it has not been shown unequivocally in adult salmon, it is assumed that they retain the same sensory abilities. A solar compass providing orientation cues is of limited use when the sun isn't visible, so an additional sense is presumably utilized, and effective navigation requires that the navigator can deduce position in the ocean as well as position relative to a destination. It is believed that adult salmon can sense and orient in the earth's geomagnetic field, a capability that has been demonstrated in some birds, bees, and other fish, even salmon fry. Exactly how the magnetoreceptive mechanism works is not known; however, tiny chains of magnetite particles have been found in the dermethoid skull bones of chinook salmon and within the lateral line of Atlantic salmon. They may function as part of a sensory system, because the magnetite particles carry their own permanent magnetic field and rotate to align with earth's magnetic field, creating a tiny yet measurable force, which is monitored by specialized nerve receptors and tissue. At critical times in its development, geomagnetic information unique to a particular location is imprinted on the salmon's memory. It can be recalled to form a piscine map of the world and to navigate to natal rivers, where other sensory modalities take over.

For salmon, finding their way back to their natal nesting site in the Salmon Forest is based on multiple navigation techniques, depending on their proximity to their destination. Once they are in the vicinity of the estuaries and rivers that will take them to their spawning grounds, the "map and compass" navigational scheme used in the open ocean gives way to navigation based primarily on olfactory cues; they begin to smell their way home. The chemical cues that enable the salmon to differentiate water originating from their natal nesting sites are too dilute once the freshwaters have been mixed in the ocean, so this olfaction-based scheme is of most use once the salmon have reached a freshwater source that provides a steady current of odors to guide them. And it is important to remember that the chemical signatures from their spawning beds are hidden within a turbulent mixture of fresh- and salt water of varying temperature and salinity and mixed with innumerable other molecules and pheromones that may attract or repel the migrating salmon. That a salmon can do this so successfully indicates that individual streams and nesting areas have unique chemical characteristics that remain stable, at least during the life cycle of the salmon, and that a salmon can actually distinguish these characteristics from those of surrounding streams. Its ability to return to its place of origin implies that a salmon must learn or imprint the chemical characteristics of its natal stream around the time of its emergence from the nest and during its downstream migration prior to and during smolting, and it requires that the salmon remember and respond to the olfactory cues when returning as an adult.

The sensory details of olfactory homing, like those of magnetoreception, are not completely understood. What chemicals are involved and their exact origin, and whether there are species- or population-specific pheromones that may have a genetic basis have not been deduced. The sensory cells responsible for chemoreception—the sense of smell—are primarily found lining the walls of invaginated pits behind the nares, which are nostril-like openings on the salmon's nose. These cells have evolved to be extremely sensitive to minute quantities of very specific chemicals; as little as a single molecule contacting the outer cell membrane triggers an electrical nervous response. This response is conducted, either by long axons on the end of the sensory cell or through a secondary nerve, directly to the olfactory bulb, a structure in the most forward part of the brain that controls the chemical perception of odors. Salmon have hundreds of thousands of odor-sensing cells in close proximity to the brain, capable of responding to a multitude of dissolved chemicals, but they must still be able to distinguish those scents particular to their natal nest sites and then coordinate their behavior.

Recent studies have shown that salmon may accomplish the imprinting of olfactory information, their "scent memory," into their sensory cells and nervous tissue in several ways. At specific times in salmon development, like when first leaving the nest or during smolting, as well as under changing environmental conditions, there is a distinct surge in the release of certain endocrine hormones from the thyroid gland. These hormone surges result in the proliferation of olfactory neurons with a sensitivity specific to scents present in the water at that time, as well as to an increased responsiveness of the individual sensor cells themselves. These cellular changes are concomitant with growth in the nerve cells within the olfactory bulb of the brain and together presumably form the base material in which to imprint a scent memory. This imprinting mechanism forms a pliant system that can be tuned to critical chemical markers in the environment present at key stages in salmon development. It also allows salmon to imprint sensory information opportunistically, in response to new environmental stimuli encountered during their early migration. Exactly how a salmon retrieves and compares its internal scent map with the olfactory information it perceives as it swims upriver—what, if anything, a salmon thinks—is of course unknown, but suffice it to say it has worked extraordinarily well for many thousands of years.

o　　o　　o

A SALMON returning to freshwater from a life in the ocean requires a change in its osmoregulatory system similar to that at smolting, but in reverse. The salmon's bodies undergo cellular and physiological changes in order to rid their systems of excess water and actively absorb the necessary ions from their environment. They also go through profound physiological modifications in preparation for reproduction. Their bodies flood with the hormones involved in gonad development, maturing their ovaries and testes and packing their bodies with eggs and sperm. These changes place an enormous requirement on the metabolism during a time of increased physical exertion, when the fish are fighting their way upstream, and during a time of starvation, because they stop feeding once they begin their spawning run. This incredible metabolic feat is made possible by the sacrificial assimilation of other body tissues; over 50 percent of the salmon's muscle protein and 90 percent of its fat are absorbed while migrating, although their body weight remains relatively constant because the missing tissue is replaced by water. Even the kidney, which is critical for osmoregulation, begins to deteriorate just as the higher physiological demands are being incurred. During these last stages of its life cycle a salmon's behavior and physiology focus only on reproduction, at the expense of all else, and lead to the genetically programmed death of the salmon on its spawning bed.

Between 95 and 99 percent of the salmon that reach reproductive age manage to return to their birth site. But what is the advantage of struggling a thousand kilometers upriver, over rushing cataracts and past a gauntlet of predators, to spawn in a place that may appear to be just like any other? An optimum nest site has water of the correct depth and suitable velocity: if the flow is too weak, the water can stagnate; if it is too strong, females may be unable to dig nests or will waste precious energy fighting the current,

and strong currents can shift sediments that may damage eggs beneath the substrate. The sediment must be of the correct size to facilitate digging and allow water to permeate the nest to flush the eggs with fresh oxygen and remove waste products. And the water itself has to be clean, clear, and well oxygenated, as well as the correct temperature to incubate the eggs. The nesting sites must also be located in areas with nearby habitat suitable for emerging alevins, as well as protected from extremes in flow that might come during times of flood or drought. By returning to the very nesting site where it was born, a salmon increases the chance of survival of its own offspring; the adult survived, ipso facto, the nesting site was a good one. And it takes two salmon to reproduce, so returning to the natal stream ensures that there are appropriate numbers of males and females present to compete for mates. In an evolutionary context, their excellence at homing strengthens the reproductive isolation of the different salmon populations, which then adapt to the environmental conditions (temperature, sediment size, flow rates, etc.) that are characteristic of their home river. An anadromous life history that includes long and complex migratory paths tends to disperse a population as well as disperse the population's gene pool over a larger area (which could be considered an advantage or a disadvantage); homing helps salmon adapt to local conditions, fine-tuning the species to optimize its chances of passing on its genes to its progeny.

There is a very small fraction of the migrating salmon population that doesn't return to its natal stream. These fish are referred to as "strays," and it is not known whether this behavior is based on an impulse by the salmon to spawn elsewhere or a failure of their homing instinct. The occasional failure or stray is actually of benefit. If homing were absolutely perfect, the population would be literally and figuratively keeping all its eggs in one basket. Unerring

return to the natal stream helps salmon populations adapt to their environment, but it puts the entire stock at risk should there be some sort of catastrophic disturbance. Should a landslide smother or divert a spawning stream, or an advancing continental ice sheet dam an entire watershed, those migrating salmon that stray allow the recolonization of other habitats and the continuation of at least some of the population. Straying salmon also allow the mixing of genes between different populations, which provides vigor to the species as a whole and is the mechanism by which salmon have naturally extended their range around the Pacific rim.

The collapse of the sockeye salmon fishery on the Fraser River in British Columbia should have been a prescient example of what can happen to salmon and other natural resources when disrupted. Between 1912 and 1914, a series of landslides initiated by railroad construction on the steep hillsides around Hells Gate, a particularly narrow gorge in the Fraser River canyon, partially dammed the river with debris. The constriction in the flow increased the velocity and turbulence in the river to such an extent that the salmon were no longer able to pass. Instead they struggled against the currents and rapids until they were exhausted and then milled about in side pools and eddies without ever reaching their nesting sites in lakes and tributaries farther upstream. During the peak sockeye spawning run in 1913, millions of sockeye were seen backed up along more than fifteen kilometers of the river below Hells Gate, and the Fraser River was crimson in places from the bodies of struggling salmon. A witness recounted, "The fish were doing their best, throwing themselves out of the water in their eagerness and wounding themselves against the rocks or the slide to get a purchase against the current" (quoted in Evenden 2004). Heroic, but mostly futile, attempts were made to aid the salmon by shuttling them by hand-dipped net and using wooden flumes to divert them around the rapids while workers struggled to remove the debris from the landslides. Despite these efforts, only a handful of fish ever reached their spawning sites. This had a devastating effect on important aboriginal fishing grounds upstream, which had been used for over four thousand years by the Nlaka'pamux and earlier First Nation tribes. At the time, the Fraser River spawning population was also the nucleus of American and Canadian commercial fisheries, which caught more than thirty million sockeye from the waters around Vancouver Island and Juan de Fuca Strait in 1913. There were over forty canneries around Vancouver on the Canadian side alone.

The catastrophe of the Hells Gate landslides, and the coincident heavy fishing pressure, is reflected in the fisheries' catches in the years after the slides. In 1917, which should have seen the return of the 1913 Fraser River offspring after four years of maturation, the catch was only one-quarter the 1913 level. By 1921 it was only one-thirtieth, and the regional sockeye salmon fishery had collapsed. However, both the salmon and the fisheries ultimately survived. The remaining Fraser River sockeye population and strays from other rivers have slowly repopulated the watershed, although it is only recently that they have returned to spawn in numbers remotely close to the those experienced prior to the collapse. The people of the region adapted as well. With the loss of their native fishery, the First Nation peoples shifted away from a salmon-based economy to one with more agriculture, hunting, and wage labor in the expanding cities and towns. The commercial fishing industry survived by shifting its focus to other salmon species, like the pink and coho; and like a straying salmon, the commercial fisheries expanded their geographic range and dispersed to begin catching fish farther and farther to the north.

∘ ∘ ∘

EVEN AFTER a migratory life as strenuous and eventful as that of a salmon—surviving thousands of kilometers of river and ocean— the final act of reproduction is anything but peaceful. Males and females both struggle until the very end in a competition for limited resources. Females must locate and then compete for the best nesting locations, and males compete for the chance to access a mate. The best nesting sites have an optimum combination of water flow and sediment size, and females aggressively defend their selected sites from intruders. Males bite, block, and bash each other in displays of physical dominance; usually the largest and best-conditioned males win. Some smaller males adopt "sneak" tactics in a clandestine mating behavior that is not unique to the kokanee; they quickly assume a coloration more similar to that of the female and slip unnoticed past larger, aggressive males and attempt to mate.

At the chosen nesting site the female rapidly flexes her tail and the side of her body against the bottom, flushing fine sediments away and digging a depression of gravel and small stones that is about eighteen to fifty centimeters deep. The entire process may take a few hours; when she is ready to release her eggs, she sinks her belly to the bottom of the nest. The ever-vigilant dominant males monitor the female behavior and the state of her nest preparations and when finally ready to spawn, they swim tightly alongside her while posturing and vibrating their bodies. Egg release by the females takes less than a minute; the males release their milt synchronously, and fertilization, the union of egg and sperm, takes place in the water column as the eggs fall down into the gravel below the spawning pair. In densely populated nesting areas, with sometimes hundreds of males vying for the opportunity to spawn, multiple males may stack up above mating pairs and simultaneously release their milt, so eggs in a nest may actually have been fertilized by more than one father.

Adult male sockeye salmon *(Oncorhynchus nerka)* fighting in shallow water. Adult males engage in fierce biting and tail slapping in order to prove dominance and establish mating access to females.

After spawning, adults are emaciated and their bodies torn and battered. The males are exhausted by competition for mates; the females guard their nests until they are too weak to hold their position in the current, then they drift away and die.

After she has released her eggs, the salmon female immediately covers the area with gravel and starts digging a new nest, just upstream of the first, and the entire spawning process begins again, until all her eggs have been shed. The entire redd may eventually consist of four or five individual nests made by the female over two or three days. Once all her eggs have been released the female patrols and protects the redd to prevent other females from digging there and disrupting her eggs, as later-arriving salmon also want to select optimum locations to spawn. She will continue her guardian duties until completely exhausted. Males continue competing for the opportunity to mate with ripe females until all remaining salmon have perished and drifted away in the current. Then their carcasses choke the shallows, get caught in streamside foliage, and rot upon the shores. Their bodies disappear quickly and there are no visible traces of the previous generation when the next spawning adults return.

The story of the salmon has come full circle: from the freshwater streams of the forest, to the open ocean, and then back to the lakes, rivers, and streams beneath the forest canopy, birth and death and life are renewed. Because of the sheer numbers of salmon returning to their birthplace, at least in times past, and because salmon achieve nearly all of their body mass while living in the sea, there is an enormous transport of biomass from the ocean to the freshwater ecosystems where they die. The salmon life cycle creates an incredible conveyor belt of nutrients and energy from marine ecosystems to terrestrial ones in a world where, typically, gravity pulls all things downhill from the mountains and deposits them in the sea. Their life history of anadromy and semelparity transports millions of tons of salmon flesh into nutrient-poor freshwaters that then shape the entire Salmon Forest. By the time the last of their watery flesh has tumbled from their bones and the last bits of their cartilage have melted into the streamside shore, they will have been preyed upon, scavenged, and decomposed by a multitude of creatures, from sharks to bears, gulls, beetles, and bacteria. All living things possess a unique gestalt, perhaps none more so than the salmon, whose life, we now see, extends far beyond the boundaries of its body, encompassing the entire forest and expanding far into the Pacific Ocean.

THE SALMON SIGNATURE

OUR ABILITY to understand and quantify the exact role of salmon in the ocean and rivers of the world, beyond what generations of naturalists, scientists, and First Nation fishermen have observed with their eyes, has relied on the development of sophisticated instrumentation that does nothing less than tear apart and weigh the primordial constituents of an organism on an atomic level. This incredible device, the mass spectrometer, has been in development for over a century as a specialized tool for probing the physics and chemistry of matter, but only in recent decades has it been refined enough for routine application in the environmental sciences. The use of this instrument to tease apart the details of an organism's relationship with the surrounding environment hinges on fundamental facts that govern all of life.

The salmon come from the stars. This is a contingent fact of our universe, the direct result of everything we know being composed of recycled star dust. The native fisherman spearing dinner, the pine trees along the river banks, the mayflies that dance for just one day in the warm sunlight above a rushing stream, the wave-worn rocks along the seashore, the air that we breathe, and the waters in which the salmon swim are all, for the most part, made of elements that were born in the hearts of stars and spewed forth when larger stars died as spectacular supernovae. The nuclear engines inside the stars formed the heavy elements like oxygen, carbon, and nitrogen from the hydrogen and helium generated during the first minutes after the big bang. The violent death of large stars has blasted these atomic elements throughout the cosmos, where they have been recycled through other stars or have coalesced into solar systems. When the conditions were just right, the elements formed the earth, liquid water, an oxygen/nitrogen atmosphere, and the blood and pink tissue of the salmon. When a salmon dies, the elements that make up its flesh are absorbed back into the ecosystem through the actions of predators and scavengers and decomposers of the forest. When our sun dies, it will most likely expand as a red giant star and vaporize the earth and then collapse upon itself to form a tiny dwarf. The gas of the expanding nebulae left behind by the dwarf, containing the elements of our sun, the earth, and the salmon, will disperse in the galaxy and be cycled again.

The main elemental building blocks of a salmon, and all other living things, are composed of carbon, hydrogen, oxygen, and nitrogen, as well as phosphorus, silicon, sulfur, and a sprinkling of other elements like chlorine, iodine, bromine, and some metals like copper and iron. The molecules that form proteins, sugars, lipids, and nucleic acids (like RNA and DNA) are composed of different combinations of these elements held together by different types of chemical bonds. These organic molecules form tissues; and these tissues are assembled into organs, whose systems all work in synchrony to form what is ultimately a swimming, jumping, feeding, and spawning salmon.

Any individual element, like carbon, or oxygen, is defined by its subatomic structure. It has a nucleus composed of positively charged protons surrounded by a cloud of negatively charged

electrons. The number of protons that an element has makes that particular element unique and gives it specific chemical properties. Carbon, for example, has six protons in its nucleus; oxygen has eight. Typically, there are equal numbers of electrons and protons in an element, providing a balance between the positive and negative charges. This charge balance is important for controlling chemical reactions and governs the making and breaking of molecular bonds between different atoms and molecules. These chemical processes are fundamental in everything around us, from controlling the way oxygen is absorbed by the bloodstream to how plants produce sugars from sunlight and how an iron fishing boat rusts while moored at the dock.

Protons and electrons are not the only particles that make up an atom. In addition to the positively charged protons, the nucleus of an atom contains particles with no charge, called neutrons, which help keep the nucleus together. Almost always, the number of neutrons in a nucleus is equal to the number of protons. However, a very small percentage of atoms have an unequal number of neutrons and protons. These are known as isotopes of a given element. The most infamous are the radioisotopes of uranium, where differences in the proton/neutron balance can lead to the emission of various subatomic particles and the radioactive decay of uranium into other elements. This radioactive decay can release energy—in a controlled form, like within a nuclear reactor, that can be used to generate electrical power, or in a less-controlled, rapid release of large amounts of energy as in an atomic bomb.

About 10 percent of the elemental isotopes are stable isotopes, which means that they do not undergo any radioactive transformation. These stable isotopes are found in everything around us and are very safe, nondecaying, and impart only extremely subtle differences to the way in which the element interacts with the chemical environment. It takes a sophisticated machine, the mass spectrometer, to detect the tiny differences in the weight of an individual atom caused by the presence or absence of a neutron in the nucleus. In the world outside the laboratory, in the world of the salmon, the effects of stable isotopes are invisible.

Even though the differences are subtle, isotopes of the same element are different in the way they react with other atoms. Isotopes with fewer neutrons, or "lighter" isotopes, typically react slightly faster than "heavier" isotopes (those with more neutrons than protons). And after a series of chemical reactions, the final chemical products tend to have fewer of those isotopes with extra neutrons (the heavier isotopes). Over long periods of time, the slight differences in the heavy/light isotope balance in the environment can create distinctive isotopic signatures. For instance, the processes of evaporation and condensation alter the isotopic composition of hydrogen and oxygen molecules in water and create different isotopic signatures for water falling as rain, evaporating from the surface of the sea, or existing in a glacier high on a mountainside. When any plant combines carbon dioxide and water in the process of photosynthesis to form simple carbohydrates (the building blocks and energy sources for much of life on earth), the chain of sunlight-powered chemical reactions increases the number of heavy carbon isotopes in the plant tissue, making them distinctive from the pools of carbon atoms in the atmospheric carbon dioxide. The well-mixed pool of nitrogen isotopes in the atmosphere can be altered by various industrial pollutants as well as by the day-to-day activities of life on earth. As organisms decompose, the remaining particulate matter that rains down to the depths of a lake or ocean floor or is mixed into the soil has a disproportionate number of heavy nitrogen isotopes. Any animal, like a salmon, eats its prey and metabolizes the nutrients and then excretes waste. At each

step in the process, the nitrogen isotopes present in animal tissues are increasingly skewed toward the heavier nitrogen isotopes. And this isotope balance is carried along throughout the food chain, with carnivores having greater numbers of heavy nitrogen isotopes than the organisms that made up their last lunch. The trail of stable isotopes can be traced from plankton in the sea through the salmon juveniles that feed on the plankton, through the wolves, foxes, bears, and birds that feed on spawning salmon, into the bacterial community feasting on the decaying carcasses of dead salmon, into the soils forming the banks of the spawning stream, and then through the roots and right to the very tops of the spruce and cedar trees growing in the surrounding Salmon Forest.

The fingerprint imparted by heavy and light isotopic ratios can often provide a remarkably detailed glimpse of an organism's life if carefully interpreted. The step-by-step enrichment of heavy nitrogen isotopes records the flow of nutrients between predators and prey. For instance, it is possible to discern the behavior of different orca populations by the weight of the nitrogen isotopes in their tissues. In the Pacific Northwest there are resident orca pods that feed almost exclusively on salmon and other fish, and their nitrogen isotopic signature is different from, and lighter than, the nitrogen signature of transient orca that also frequent the region but feed exclusively on other marine mammals. The transient orca have distinctly heavier nitrogen isotopic ratios because they prey upon animals, for instance, sea lions, that have preyed upon the salmon and already enriched their heavy isotope ratio during their metabolism. Eating the sea lion further enriches the nitrogen in the transient orca.

Salmon are particularly useful for isotopic study because their life history imparts a unique stamp to their tissue nitrogen and carbon isotopic ratios. Because they no longer eat once they begin

Orca *(Orcinus orca)* are apex predators and iconic symbols of the Pacific Northwest. They are sophisticated hunters and a full-grown adult can consume hundreds of kilograms of fish daily.

their spawning run, their body tissues have an isotopic signature that reflects their marine origin and is relatively frozen in place. Nitrogen is an essential nutrient for all life forms, and by measuring the quantity of different nitrogen isotopes in a tissue, the source of the nutrients can be deduced. Most terrestrial sources of nitrogen ultimately come from bacterial microorganisms that are capable of synthesizing, or "fixing," nitrogen-rich ammonia from the gaseous nitrogen in the atmosphere. These microorganisms tend to live symbiotically with other animals, like termites, or within specialized growths on certain plants. In the Pacific Northwest, the alder trees *(Alnus incana, A. rubra)* have a symbiotic relationship with the nitrogen-fixing bacterium *(Frankia alni)* that grows in special nodules within the trees' root system. The bacteria absorb nitrogen from the air, then provide it to the tree in the form of ammonia, which is created using specific anaerobic enzymes unique to the bacteria. The tree reciprocates by providing energy to the bacteria, in the form of carbon compounds produced from photosynthesis, and it provides the bacteria with a protective, oxygen-free microenvironment within the nodule that allows the bacteria to flourish. The isotopic signature incorporated in a

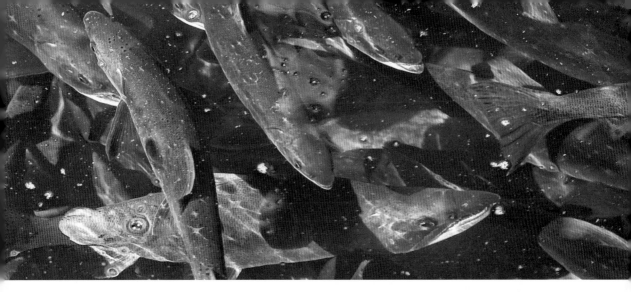

tissue via this terrestrial nitrogen nutrient pathway is very different than the signature captured within the body of a salmon. By examining the isotopic ratio of these tracer elements from any organic sample, whether it be from detritus in the soil, the flesh of an eagle, or the leaves from a treetop, it is possible to conclude whether those nutrients came from the land or from the sea.

In essence, our salmon spend their lives swimming in waters of subtly varying isotopic composition. A scientist can read these hidden chemical messages and can tell a story—of what the fish have eaten and where, and where the body of the salmon has cycled through the entire ecosystem. It is not an easy tale to decode; over geologic time scales, specific isotopic combinations reach steady states in different parts of the physical environment. Then biologic processes—Tennyson's "Nature, red in tooth and claw"—metabolism, photosynthesis, decomposition, the physiology of growth and development, all the things that make a salmon a salmon, serve to mix these sorted isotopic signatures. However, once the isotopic tale is understood, it tells the story of how a fish is intimately linked with both the sea and the land and truly is more than the sum of its parts.

T O A BIOLOGIST, describing a salmon's gestalt is actually a question of accurately defining the salmon's niche. The term *niche* implies more to a scientist than the common notions of a niche as being something's particularly suitable position in the idiomatic grand scheme of things. In scientific parlance, a salmon's niche can have quantifiable characteristics, and it is an ecological construct of subtle meaning that was debated for decades. Informal thoughts of an organism's niche had been considered for many years, but this important biological concept wasn't unequivocally stated until about 1920, by the zoologist Joseph Grinnell. To Grinnell, a niche was an idealized concept of physical space; it was an indication of a geographical distribution with limits, restricted by physical or climatic barriers that were particular to different species. The salmon's physical world is restricted to the freshwaters of the coastal forests, as well as the pelagic Pacific Ocean. On a finer scale, you can place further limits on this potentially enormous environmental space by considering other variables, like a salmon's requirements for water of a specific temperature, or amount of dissolved oxygen, or salinity. The niche can be further refined by including seasonal changes in distribution, or time of day, or the variation in distribution of different life history stages.

The physical niche of an alevin is much different from that of a smolt or an adult, and all these "niche spaces" would be distinct for different salmon species.

Around the same time that this spatial conceptualization of an organism's niche was being developed, the biologist Charles Elton proposed a niche concept that implied functionality: the role that an organism plays in its community, and most important, its place as either predator or prey (i.e., its trophic status). A more subtle distinction within the niche concept is that Elton's niche represented an *actual* place in an ecosystem due to organism interaction, as opposed to the *potential* physical place in a landscape inherent in Grinnell's. This functional niche is still fluid and changes over an organism's life history; an alevin, hidden in the gravel and feeding off its yolk, has a different role in the Salmon Forest than does a planktivorous smolt in an estuary, or an adult salmon at sea feeding on squid or being snatched from a stream by a bear.

In 1932, the Russian ecologist Georgii Gause used the functional niche concept as a key component in formulating the competitive exclusion principle, which became an important axiom of modern ecology. In an elegant way, the principle states that if the characteristics defining the niche of two species are similar, the two species cannot coexist. This apparently simple axiom synthesizes the competition for limited environmental resources between populations of different species, the evolutionary powers of natural selection, with the idea of a niche as a functional unit. Should there be two or more species competing for the same resources, like food or space, whichever species has even the slimmest competitive advantage will eventually prevail over the others. Only one species can occupy that ecological niche, and the others are either driven to extinction or must adapt their behavior and evolve to occupy a slightly different one.

A brown bear *(Ursus arctos)* proves itself a talented hunter and strong swimmer, capturing a salmon from a raging cataract.

In 1957, the particularly astute polymath freshwater ecologist G. Evelyn Hutchinson amalgamated the two niche interpretations—the environmental distribution of an organism versus the functional role of an organism, and the underlying themes of defining attributes of a species versus defining attributes of species interactions within an ecosystem—into a less ambiguous mathematical construct. To Hutchinson, a niche was a multidimensional space consisting of the near-infinite number of environmental variables (physical or biological), each represented as a set of axes coordinates affecting any particular species. For any distinct set of variable coordinates there are limiting values within which a species can survive and reproduce. Taken all together, the multidimensional volume constrained by the limits imposed by physical and biological factors (like temperature tolerance or preferred food size) is considered to be an animal's *fundamental niche* and completely defines its ecological properties. However, because an organism lives in a community of other organisms that it interacts with, certain parts of its fundamental niche may be regularly excluded. The reduced volume of the fundamental niche that is occupied by a population of organisms competing with other species for common resources is the *realized niche.* As an example, both adult salmon and adult hake *(Merluccius productus)* can feed on the north Pacific krill *(Euphausia pacifica),* but if either is a more capable predator (whether due to sheer numbers or to being at a more advantageous part of its life cycle), the less competitive will have to shift its feeding to a different prey species, or perhaps to krill residing in a different part of the water column, or to feeding at a different time of day not exploited by the other— hence the reduced volume in its realized niche. Although the fundamental and realized niches are purely theoretical concepts, their implementation has made quantitative niche theory an important component of modern ecological science.

The brilliance of Hutchinson wasn't his quantitative amalgamation of niche concepts. Instead, it was his use of these ideas to consider how relationships between species affect the coexistence of organisms in different ecosystems and affect the overall diversity of species present in a community. Hutchinson wrote a series of charming and now classic essays pondering what seemed to be simple ecological questions. After considering the banal presence of water bugs in a cave-side pond in Italy, he could broaden his exposition to ask, Why are there so many different kinds of animals? Why is it that some environments only support a very few species? And (in his famous "Paradox of the Plankton") why would we find such diversity of life in an environment that seems very homogenous and limited in the amount of available resources, like the planktonic midwaters of the ocean or a lake, all in seeming contradiction to Gause's axiom of competitive exclusion? This same contemplation can be applied to the Salmon Forest. Why is it that there are seven species of Pacific salmon, many with overlapping ranges? Why aren't there just one or two? or twenty?

There are a multitude of reasons why the Salmon Forest ecosystem is as diverse as it is. Often when a particular environment is examined in closer detail, what appears to be a homogenous habitat turns out to be highly variable in space and time. There are gradients in light and temperature and nutrients even in what appears to be an evenly mixed environment like the open ocean or lake, and all manner of organisms have adapted to exploit those differences. One of the reasons there are so many different types of plankton is that there is a myriad of ways that organisms have evolved to accommodate the subtle variations in that seemingly invariant realm, so that none have realized niches that completely overlap. The slowly diverging subpopulations of kokanee in Lake Kronotsky on the Kamchatka Peninsula provide another example. Two different forms of kokanee now coexist because they have diverged in their use of the same spawning grounds (one population spawning before the other) and preferentially feed on different prey in the lake. The evolved niche differentiation has reduced competition between the two populations, which might otherwise drive one population to extinction. Fish and many animals partition their environment according to size-selective feeding; they can coexist because even though they appear similar in most of their ecological attributes, they eat prey of different size. Seed-eating birds of all types, coyotes and wolves, salmon and whitefish, black bears and grizzlies all have overlapping ranges but can coexist because they prey upon slightly different resources: different sizes, or in different locations, or at different times of day. The fact that all habitats, whether they are marine or terrestrial, have constantly fluctuating environmental and ecological conditions and never quite reach an eternally stable equilibrium that would favor one competing species over any other, helps ensure a diverse biotic landscape. Ultimately, there are coho, sockeye, pink—all the Pacific salmon sharing many similar traits—coexisting because the adaptations of these species have evolved in close synchrony and are precisely tuned with the Pacific Northwest landscape. And, as we know, the physical landscape of the Salmon Forest is a marvelous tapestry of terrains, where just a few kilometers can span habitats that range from cold alpine slopes, to grassy meadows, to towering rain forest. A single river can tumble from a chill mountain cataract, through swift courses broken by pools and lakes, to the warm lazy meander of a swampy wetland along a coastal estuary, and out into the open sea. During the course of its life, a single salmon may inhabit them all.

∘   ∘   ∘

THE SCIENTIFIC STUDY of ecology (from the Greek οἶκος-λογία, quite literally, "the study of our house") as an examination of how all living things interact with each other and their surroundings is not a modern discipline. Aristotle and many other ancient philosophers were cognizant of an interconnection between organisms and their environment, but it wasn't until Charles Darwin published *On the Origin of Species* in 1859 that adaptation by way of natural selection provided a mechanism and evolutionary processes provided a context for ecological, if not all biological, theory. Until then, the study of ecology tended to be observational, and even though some studies considered more modern themes, like the regulation of organism population size, environmental gradients and resultant organism distributions, and so on, it wasn't until Darwin and postulates of natural selection that scientists began to understand the reciprocal interactions between organisms and the environment. This was a major paradigm shift in biological thinking and shapes all modern theory. In the context of evolution, ecology is embedded with organism physiology, genetics, behavior, and the physical characteristics of the surrounding environment.

"The study of our house," *oekologie,* was coined by German morphologist/philosopher Ernst Haeckel in 1866. Haeckel was an ardent follower of the works of the famous and prolific taxonomist Carl Linnaeus, and Haeckel's concept of ecology fused Linnaean ideas of the "polity of nature" with newfound evolutionism. To Linnaeus the natural world was entwined with the divine, and the relationships between organisms and their environment were part of a holistic view of how God and nature existed in equilibrium. Haeckel declared that the study of ecology should "investigate the total relations of the animal both to its inorganic and to its organic environment; including, above all, its friendly and inimical relations with those animals and plants with which it comes directly or indirectly into contact—in a word, ecology is the study of all those complex interrelations referred to by Darwin as the conditions of the struggle for existence" (quoted in Allee et al. 1949). Haeckel sought to elaborate the rigorous approach of studying organism physiology by advocating to include the relationship between organisms and their physical and biological surroundings in the context of Darwinian evolution. His *oekologie* marked, then, a critical juncture in theories of how species are created—not in an environmental vacuum, but via dynamic selection, within all of nature, as Darwin emphasized. The term *ecosystem* wasn't defined until the 1930s, to expressly describe a complete environmental unit, or system, that includes not only all the organisms in the biological community but also all aspects of the physical environment that the organisms interact within, and everything that contributes to the flow of energy and cycling of nutrients. Simply, an ecosystem includes the entire biological community as well as the complex physical environment; and ecology is the study of ecosystems.

Central to the study of the Salmon Forest, and all ecosystems, is tracking the utilization and flow of energy within them. In nearly every ecosystem on earth, including those which the salmon traverse, all the energy ultimately comes from the sun. In just over eight minutes, photons generated tens of thousands of years ago deep within our sun streak across the interplanetary medium and intercept the earth. This sunlight generates our planet's weather and climate, drives the circulation of the oceans, and is the root source of power for the Salmon Forest.

The least complicated way to consider the energy flow through the ecosystem is as a linear food chain. This is the archaic, yet nonetheless useful, notion that an ecosystem's energy can be summarized in a progressive series of "what eats what" predator-prey interactions, with definitive beginnings and ends. All such chains begin with autotrophs, plants and phytoplankton mostly, which are able to manufacture their own food via photosynthesis. These primary producers use the light from the sun to make simple sugars by combining water and carbon dioxide, effectively converting solar energy into chemical potential energy in a general process referred to as carbon fixation. The simple photosynthetic sugars, along with additional critical nutrients, form the building blocks of what eventually become complex molecules like carbohydrates, proteins, and other polysaccharides through an incredible series of biosynthetic pathways operating within living cells. The next organisms along a food chain must acquire the energy to survive by consuming autotrophs. These are heterotrophs, which are at least two biologic steps removed from the energy of the sun, and by digesting primary producers like ocean phytoplankton or the succulent leaves of a streamside bush, they gain both the energy needed to power their own metabolism and a source of "pre-fixed" carbon building blocks that they can utilize in their own biosynthetic pathways. The heterotrophs that specialize in eating only autotrophs are known as herbivores and "primary consumers." Heterotrophs that specialize in consuming other heterotrophs, specifically herbivores, are known as carnivores, or "secondary consumers." "Tertiary consumers" are predatory carnivores that prey upon both herbivores and other carnivores. Salmon tend to be tertiary consumers in aquatic ecosystems because they prey upon zooplankton (which graze on the primary producer phytoplankton) as well as upon invertebrates and other small fishes, which in turn have been preying upon other herbivorous or carnivorous creatures. At the very end of the food chain are the apex predators—organisms that exist usually in relatively low numbers and that have no predators of their own. In the Pacific Northwest, the brown or grizzly bear and the orca are the quintessential apex predators.

The *troph* in heterotroph and autotroph implies nourishment, and ecologists refer to the collection of organisms that are all at the same number of predatory steps away from the primary producers as being on the same trophic level. There tends to be a maximum number of trophic levels that any ecosystem can support; there can be only so many links in a food chain. This is because the transfer of energy from trophic level to trophic level is never 100 percent efficient, and therefore not all the potential energy contained in a prey item is available to a predator. If a bear wades into a stream and catches a salmon, only about 10 percent of the chemical energy stored in the salmon's flesh is transferred to the bear to support its metabolism. Often it is much less. The remaining 90 percent (or more) of the energy is "lost" from the ecosystem as heat or waste, yet another consequence of the entropic thermodynamics and the tendency for randomness in the universe. Because each link in the predator-prey chain, from phytoplankton to brown bear, loses so much of the original solar energy to entropy, the length of the food chain, or the number of trophic levels, is usually only four or five. Marine ecosystems can support a higher number of trophic levels because the transfer of energy from phytoplankton to some zooplankton grazers can sometimes be as much as 40 percent efficient. As a consequence of the loss of energy up through the trophic tiers of the Salmon Forest, the numbers and biomass of organisms living at each tropic level decrease,

Swimming in Lynn Canal, Alaska, a member of a small pod of orca patrols the inshore waters. There are three races of orca in the Pacific Northwest. The "resident" race tends to follow salmon migratory patterns, as salmon make up the bulk of its diet.

Setting nets in the Gastineau Channel near Juneau, Alaska. Modern fishing techniques are extremely efficient and easily outcompete even the most effective natural predators for salmon prey.

creating a trophic pyramid with only a few apex predators at top, supported by a broad base of autotrophs. Every salmon that survives to spawn has been supported by energy transmuted by many hundreds of thousands, if not millions, of organisms in lower trophic groups. And likewise, the energy to sustain every bear or wolf or orca in the Pacific Northwest can only come from countless salmon and the salmon's trophic brethren.

Although considering the role of organisms as components in a linear food chain or trophic hierarchy is demonstrative when considering gross ecosystem energy flow, it is unfortunately not a strictly accurate depiction of nature. In the real world, animals prey upon many different species that may exist in different trophic levels, and those predators themselves are eaten by many different other species, not just one in a linear fashion. The trophic relationships can change with time of day, time of year, and the stage of an organism's development. Omnivores, like bears, can prey on higher trophic levels or graze on autotrophic grasses. And a salmon feeds on lower trophic levels as an alevin, feeds simultaneously on multiple prey organisms as an adult, stops feeding altogether when spawning, and at any time during its life cycle is victim to various viruses and parasites that don't fit easily into the food chain concept.

In the 1920s several ecologists championed the idea of a food *web* to describe the interconnectedness of organisms in their environment. Charles Elton, while not only formulating early conceptions of an organism's niche, also helped propose the food web as a series of intertwined and overlapping food chains that when synthesized help capture the intricacies of organisms and the ecosystem. Energy flows not just up a chain from autotroph to heterotroph, but between chains of different species, in an increasingly complex network. The ecosystem of an entire community, like the

Salmon Forest, or the African savannah, or a landlocked lake, was then best considered as an assemblage of trophic webs that maps the flow of energy throughout.

In the case of the Salmon Forest the trophic webs connect many species, but the salmon are such a critical component in so many different webs that they form an important nexus between both terrestrial and aquatic communities. Salmon are linked to marine and freshwater ecosystems where they spawn, develop, and mature and to the terrestrial forest when fed upon by a multitude of animals when they return to their natal streams to spawn and die. There are additional trophic webs, more cryptic in nature. There are an enormous number of detritivores in the community, organisms specialized to feed on dead organic matter. Beetles, flies, and their larvae, as well as bacteria and fungi, feed on the bounty of salmon carcasses, decomposing the bodies and helping return the flesh and bone of what was once a fish to simple molecules and nutrients that are integrated into the watershed. In addition, the detritivores are then eaten by an equally enormous number of other organisms at higher trophic levels, forming their own detrital food web. More hidden still is a vast network of single-celled organisms, like algae and protozoa, bacteria and viruses, that form the microbial trophic web and recycle dissolved carbon, hence energy, between the physical environment and higher trophic levels.

In fact, the importance of salmon to the detrital and microbial food webs is so great that it has been shown that rivers and streams that receive a large number of salmon carcasses show higher growth rates and greater numbers of hatching and developing salmon the following season. Watersheds devoid of salmon show lower productivity; the forests are not as dense or quick growing, the number of species living beneath and within the green canopy is not as diverse, because the interconnected food webs of the forest lack the pulse of energy the salmon bring. Each year anadromous salmon transport many tons of marine-derived nutrients and carbon into the freshwater and terrestrial realms, and the nutrients, vital minerals, and more complex biomolecules contained in the salmon body enrich freshwater ecosystems typically low in important nutrients like nitrogen and phosphorus and sustain many different trophic levels. Salmon streams support higher numbers of aquatic and terrestrial insects and other zooplankton invertebrates. These in turn support the vast community of small fishes and larger invertebrates that sustain salmon young as they grow, forming a positive feedback loop. Living and dying salmon enrich their ecosystem, benefiting future salmon populations and increasing the productivity and diversity of the Salmon Forest in a wonderful self-sustaining cycle.

After examining numerous communities around the world, ecologists documented an interesting relationship between trophic web complexity and the stability of ecosystems. Stability in this case implies the relative long-term continuity of the flora and fauna as well as the capability of a community to withstand perturbations, and ecosystems that show a great diversity and interconnectedness in trophic structure show the greatest stability. Presumably this arises because a diverse network of connections between organisms and the environment provides numerous counterbalancing ecological influences that together engineer a stable system. Why this is so is actually paradoxical.

(Overleaf) A rich coastal ecosystem has a diversity of habitats. The ecological engineering that results from salmon spawning can transform a watershed in many ways, from affecting the growth of adjacent forest plants to altering the course and character of entire waterways.

Ecologists examining the theoretical aspects of food web complexity have shown that, at least mathematically, such network complexity should have just the opposite effect on an ecosystem—it should make it highly unstable. In mathematical models of complex systems, disturbances to the trophic structure by the loss of a species or the disruption of a critical resource cascade and amplify throughout the entire system, causing extinction. Why this is not the case in nature may be because the spatial and temporal frameworks of the early models don't adequately reflect the subtleties of environmental variation and the nonrandom way that subsets of the entire ecosystem's trophic network assemble and reorganize as animal populations grow and migrate. Complex natural trophic networks show that certain organisms and energy pathways are compartmentalized into relatively independent subnetworks by body size or location. A deer in the forest has a tighter degree of connectedness with certain organisms, like browsable streamside grasses and shrubbery, than does, say, a bald eagle, even though they coexist in the Salmon Forest. Certain organisms—like the salmon—form focal points in trophic webs around which many other species cluster and share connectivity. As long as the highly connected species are protected, the effects of disturbances are dampened by the large number of trophic links and the compartmentalization of pathway subsets, limiting disruption to just a portion of the community.

In 1966, after examining just these sorts of relationships among intertidal organisms living along the rocky coast of Washington

Off the coast of much of the Pacific Northwest, forests of giant kelp *(Macrocystis pyrifera)* reach from the shallow sea floor toward the sunlight. These kelps are among the fastest growing of all organisms (expanding by up to half a meter per day), and their thick canopies harbor a thriving, complex ecosystem. ▶

Nestled in kelp fronds, a young sea otter *(Enhydra lutris)* rests and grooms. Sea otters are a critical species in kelp forest communities, preying on kelp-grazing sea urchins and preventing the destruction of kelp forests.

State, ecologist Robert Paine developed the keystone species concept, which has become an important component in community ecology and the management of ecosystems. Along the shore, a marine snail *(Tegula funebralis)*, a predatory starfish *(Pisaster ochraceus)*, barnacles *(Balanus* sp.), mussels *(Mytilius californianus)*, urchins *(Strongylocentrotus purpuratus)*, and a suite of brown and red algae all compete for space among the wave-swept cliffs and boulders. By carefully removing certain species from the intertidal zone and monitoring the resulting changes in remaining species' abundance and distribution, Paine could see that one species in particular, the starfish, though it occurred only in low numbers, had an enormous impact on the structure of the entire community. Removing the few starfish from an area released the feeding pressure on other species, like the snails, barnacles, and mussels, which were normally consumed by the starfish. Without this predation, certain species, like the mussels, would overwhelm the others, outcompeting them for space and radically changing the entire intertidal ecosystem.

The starfish was deemed a keystone species, one without which the ecosystem could not support itself, just like the critical keystone brick in a cathedral archway. Keystone species are those whose impact on an ecosystem is very great, and disproportionately so relative to their number in the community. These species are critical for the maintenance of the ecosystem because they interact so strongly with the dominant organisms that provide the central energy flow and community structure. Keystone species can be found in many terrestrial and aquatic ecosystems. Another example germane to the Pacific Northwest is the role of the sea otter *(Enhydra lutris)* in maintaining the health of kelp forests throughout the region. Sea otters prey upon urchins that live along the rocky seafloor and within the kelp forest. Urchins are herbivores that can graze on the base of giant kelps, and unless their numbers are reduced by feeding otters, an exploding urchin population can chew its way through the kelp holdfasts that keep the entire kelp forest canopy in place. Without an anchor, the kelps drift away and die, destroying a vast community of fishes and invertebrates that relies on the three-dimensional structure of the kelp forest for habitat. What is left behind is aptly named an "urchin barren."

F THERE ever were an iconic image of the Pacific Northwest it would be the picture of a mature bear, deftly fishing salmon from a raging cataract in the heart of the forest. This is a vision of an enormous apex predator intimately linked with its aquatic prey, and in a broad sense, an easily conceptualized intersection of the marine and terrestrial realms. And as much as the salmon's final spawning journey is an incredible feat of power and stamina, the ability of a bear to snatch a leaping fish from the air or to hunt fish darting through the water is an equally astounding display of dexterous grace.

Both black bears *(Ursus americanus)* and brown bears *(Ursus arctos)* are important inhabitants of the Salmon Forest, and because of their size, they are the most visible terrestrial consumers of spawning salmon. Both bears and salmon are keystone species; the loss of either would cause disproportionately large changes to the productivity and structure of the forest. Their trophic linkage highlights the importance of organisms that bridge normal

◀ Bears are remarkably fast and agile despite their size. They are omnivorous, and although they derive most of their diet from plants, bears seasonally feast on salmon in the Pacific Northwest.

ecosystem boundaries, like those between land and sea, and emphasizes that it is complex organism interactions that can shape the structure of communities, not just the actions of single keystone species.

Both bear species are classic omnivores and feed across multiple trophic levels; however, greater than 80 percent of their diet consists of plant material like berries, roots, nuts, grasses, and tree shoots. They also eat insects, small mammals, and rodents, scavenge carcasses from other predators, and occasionally prey upon juvenile and adult ungulates like deer, moose, elk, and bison. And in the Pacific Northwest, both black and brown bears feast on salmon. The larger, more powerful brown bear is more likely to prey upon large mammals than the smaller black bear, and in doing so has a greater influence on the population structure of herbivores and other mammals in forest and grassland ecosystems.

Although their ranges overlap, brown and black bears tend to avoid direct competition for habitat and resources; brown bears prefer higher elevations and less densely forested habitat. In Alaska and British Columbia, valleys and large offshore islands tend to have either black bears or brown bears; they very seldom have both species. Where they do co-occur, black bears tend to be subordinate to brown bears, and they divide their preferred habitat spatially and temporally to prevent encounters and competition. For the most part they are solitary animals, but they will aggregate and feed with conspecifics when food is concentrated and plentiful, like during a salmon run. Bears with access to a salmon watershed are on average larger than bears restricted to the interior of the continent, and they show a higher survivorship and greater number of cubs, presumably because of the seasonal occurrence of such an excellent food source. The availability of a high-energy food, like the lipid-rich salmon, is particularly beneficial in

the autumn, when bears begin an intense period of consumption in order to build their internal fat reserves prior to winter pseudohibernation and birthing. As a consequence of these benefits, the coastal regions of North America that have active salmon runs can support bear populations up to eighty times denser than those found in the continental interior.

Bear predation is a source of natural selection on spawning salmon. In small streams and rivers bears can consume a large enough portion of the returning adults to affect the fitness of the local salmon population. To acquire the most food energy with the least amount of effort, bears target large fish that have yet to spawn. An effect of this is that in those streams with heavy bear predation, salmon tend to be smaller and spawn earlier. It is also believed that bear predation can effect changes in salmon morphology. In those salmon species in which the spawning males develop pronounced dorsal humps, like the pink and sockeye salmon, and spawn in small, shallow, heavily predated streams, the dorsal hump is of relatively smaller size than in those streams without much bear predation. The male's dorsal hump presumably acts as a secondary sexual cue and aids sexual selection by females, and it may also function to protect males during their fights for dominance at the spawning sites. A large hump makes it more difficult for a competing male to bite across the salmon body, but a large hump makes it easier for a hunting bear to find and snatch a salmon from a shallow stream. These salmon have evolved and developed a morphotype that is a balance between these two selective pressures.

It is the bears' feeding habits that make them such critical keystone species in terrestrial communities. They are prodigious diggers, and their rooting of soils while foraging for succulent plant roots and tubers is important for mixing nutrients like nitrogen

throughout the soil. Their feeding has also been shown to increase the diversity of plants growing in an area because their disruption of the soil removes some spatially dominant plant types and allows other species to grow in their place. And the seeds of some fruit-bearing plant species only germinate after they have been partially digested and passed through the gastrointestinal tract of an animal like a bear. But it is their connection to salmon that makes the role of bears in the Pacific Northwest so profoundly important.

An average chum salmon contains about 20 grams of phosphorus, 130 grams of nitrogen, and tens of thousands of kilojoules of potential chemical energy stored in its fat and muscle tissue. If one considers the many millions of salmon that return to terrestrial watersheds, it is easy to see how this results in the transfer of thousands of tons of these essential nutrients from the ocean to the land. Salmon migrate to their natal streams, spawn, and then die, and they would transfer some of their marine-derived nutrients to the forest even without the presence of bears. However, because of the bears' feeding behavior, energy is transferred up through different trophic levels and away from the streamside, so that other organisms benefit from the salmon even if they cannot consume the fish directly.

Bears are remarkably adept at catching fish, particularly when salmon reach high densities along their spawning migration. Along one watershed black bears caught between 50 and 90 percent of the salmon entering the stream and consumed an average of thirteen fish per day per bear, and brown bears may consume even more. The energy and potential nutrients in the fish are then transferred from the water's edge to the forest as feces, urine, and partially consumed carcasses. Bears prefer to eat only the most energetically valuable parts of the salmon to maximize their feeding efficiency. After catching a fish, they typically bite through the top of the skull and consume the brain tissues and a portion of the dorsal musculature. If a female salmon has been captured, the lipid-rich eggs are pushed from the body and eaten and then the abdominal cavity is torn open to expose any remaining eggs for consumption. The male salmon's testes are not eaten because they are primarily composed of difficult-to-digest nucleic acids with little high-energy lipid content. Bears wish to avoid potentially hazardous confrontations with other bears and will carry their prey away from the spawning stream and deeper into the forest for consumption if other bears are present. After they have eaten the most

Black bears feast on salmon on Anan Creek, Alaska. Although most bears tend to be solitary and avoid potentially hazardous confrontations with others, when food is plentiful during the peak of the salmon migration, prime fishing locations attract many bears that remain focused on feasting and not on aggressive behavior toward each other.

nutritious parts, the remainder of the carcass, which is usually more than two-thirds of the salmon's tissue, is abandoned on the forest floor, where it is then available to different organisms at other trophic levels, from scavenging rodents, birds, and small mammals to insects, worms, microbes, and other detrital decomposers.

Gray wolves *(Canis lupus)*, like most of the Canidae (including foxes and coyotes), are masterful opportunists. Although they typically feed on deer and other ungulate animals, wolves are capable of eating just about anything. Wolves range across much of the northern hemisphere, and where their pack territories overlap the Salmon Forest watershed, they are known to feed upon salmon, catching live adults and scavenging postspawning carcasses. Where salmon are available, feeding on them can provide an adaptive benefit to the wolves, and salmon-derived nutrients have been identified in scat and tissue samples taken from wolves in the interior of Alaska and Canada, more than 1,000 kilometers from the sea. This isn't surprising; the Yukon River drainage covers more than 845,000 square kilometers, and each year more than two million salmon migrate into this river system to spawn, some traveling as far as 3,000 kilometers upriver.

Salmon are a seasonally abundant, predictable resource that is exploited by wolves, particularly if ungulate prey are unavailable. Salmon biomass can support wolf populations in interior regions in almost as high a density as in those areas that have much greater numbers of their preferred ungulate prey. Also, pursuing and attacking large, potentially dangerous mammals like deer, moose, and caribou is inherently hazardous to the wolves,

Although wolves *(Canis lupus)* typically prey on deer and other ungulates, the salmon migration provides an additional food source capable of supporting large wolf populations in areas that lack a sufficient supply of their usual mammal prey. ▶

Coyote *(Canis latrans)*.

whereas preying on salmon imposes much less risk to the hunters. Like bears, wolves preferentially consume only some parts of the salmon and leave the remaining carcass on the forest floor. They tend to eat only the head of the fish, and this may be because when food is abundant they can afford to target the energetically rich body parts, like the lipid-packed brain, and discard the rest, which is quickly consumed by scavengers and enriches the soil. And feeding exclusively on the heads might help wolves avoid infection from *Neorickettsia* bacteria that are transmitted by parasitic trematodes thought to be concentrated in the salmon muscle and kidneys. The *Neorickettsia* bacteria causes "salmon poisoning disease," which is fatal to wolves and other canids.

Like the wolf, the coyote (*Canis latrans*), on facing page, is a canid carnivore, and although it primarily feeds upon small mammals, it has a highly adaptable diet. Its dietary flexibility plus its ability to adjust to nearly any natural or human habitat has allowed it to expand its range over most of the North American continent. Wolves are predators of coyotes, and where their ranges overlap, coyote populations are much reduced and coyotes modify their niche to avoid confrontation. In Pacific Northwest coastal forests and even urban settings, coyotes actively scavenge salmon carcasses, and, like wolves, exploit the seasonally abundant food source and transfer the energy and marine nutrients into other trophic pathways of the forest.

Important terrestrial predators of the salmon that help shape the Pacific Northwest ecosystems are not limited to the many mammals inhabiting the region. Birds too are part of the interconnected web of life that ties the ocean to the land; when wing-borne, they can spread that connection far across the continents. The bald eagle *(Haliaeetus leucocephalus)* is just one of many birds and mammals that time their migratory movements or breeding season to coincide with salmon spawning runs, but its large size and bold visage makes it an especially conspicuous part of the Salmon Forest. The predictable bounty generated by the spawning salmon is important for over one hundred bird species. The less prominent forest passerines (songbirds and other perching birds) are found in higher numbers in forests with salmon streams because these watersheds have a much higher density of terrestrial and aquatic insects, which feed on salmon carcasses and then serve as prey to the avian fauna. Gulls are prominent transient visitors to salmon-running streams and estuaries in the autumn due to their sheer numbers and raucous behavior. They congregate in the thousands during their southward migration from northern breeding grounds and gorge on drifting salmon eggs and salmon carcasses to gain the energy they require for migration and molting. Gulls alone can consume from 10 to 25 percent of the total salmon carcass biomass and from 7 to 35 percent of the salmon egg biomass; in doing so they generate thousands of tons of nitrogen- and phosphorus-enriched guano, effectively fertilizing the landscape with marine-derived nutrients.

The bald eagle, with its wingspan of up to two meters, requires a large food supply, particularly if it overwinters in northern climes. Populations of eagles tend to be food-limited in the winter months, and a study on Amchitka Island in Alaska discovered that greater than 90 percent of all eagles die, mostly of starvation, before reaching maturity. The availability of salmon carcasses is the most important factor that controls eagle distribution in the Pacific Northwest. Eagles can hunt small live salmon and other fishes, snatching them from shallow water on the fly, but they primarily scavenge carcasses whenever they are available. A single large salmon carcass can provide nourishment for up to six eagles per day, and because they are strong enough to tear through tough salmon

Bald eagles *(Haliaeetus leucocephalus)* time their migration to coincide with the spawning of the salmon. The presence of salmon carcasses is the most important factor in eagle distribution and abundance in the Pacific Northwest.

Along Pack Creek, Alaska, an eagle tears into a salmon carcass. A salmon bounty increases the survivorship rate of chicks and fledglings.

skin and dismember the skeleton, eagles are important in providing other scavengers, like crows and gulls, access to carrion. In the weeks and months after a spawning run, as the carcasses decay and become less numerous, the competition between eagles for the remaining food supply intensifies, and the most successful eagles steal the majority of their food from each other in aerial thieving, rather than scavenging along the ground. When salmon are plentiful the forest supports more nesting and breeding eagle pairs, and they are able to lay their eggs and incubate earlier in the season. This is an important advantage; not only does a greater food supply increase the survivorship of eggs and chicks, it also allows juveniles to fledge earlier in the year, giving them more time to mature and acquire the skills they need to survive the following winter.

To the Haida and other northwestern First Nation tribes, the raven, a ubiquitous presence within the Salmon Forest, is a revered mythical figure of dual character, both trickster and benevolent helper of the people. The young raven brought forth the sun, moon, and stars, covered the land with trees and lakes, created the tides, and filled the forests with animals and the rivers with salmon. Northern raven *(Corvus corax)* are highly intelligent and can be found across the entire northern hemisphere, forming large flocks when young and defending territories as mated pairs later in life. In the Salmon Forest they flourish as opportunistic omnivores, feeding on everything from berries and grains to insects, small rodents, and amphibians, and scavenging all types of carrion, particularly salmon during the spawning migration. Where salmon are abundant it is difficult to find any creature that inhabits the region that is not in some way touched by the presence of this fish.

The actions of bears, and those of wolves and raven, foxes, coyotes, and the myriad other terrestrial predators facilitate the transfer of nutrients from the ocean into the forest through the

In the mythology of First Nation peoples, the raven *(Corvus corax)* was both benevolent and a trickster. Opportunistic predators, ravens feed on salmon carcasses during spawning migrations.

spreading and subsequent breakdown of salmon carcasses, as well as by the deposition of their feces and urine after eating salmon. The high levels of nitrogen and phosphorus in these by-products of normal bear and predator activity then leach into the soil and are made available as fertilizer to the forest's primary producers. This is essential because the majority of plants and trees are unable to access nitrogen directly from the atmosphere. The overall impact of this trophic linkage between salmon, bears, and the forest is very complex. The total effect varies from year to year and season to season depending upon the numbers of returning salmon and on the spatial distribution of the bears and their territories. Some streams are not populated by bears, and part of the role of carcass transfer from the water's edge into the forest may be accomplished by other species, like wolves and eagles, whereas other streams are favorite fishing areas and hot spots for bears, and therefore hot spots for bear-mediated nutrient transfer. Decomposing carcasses in the water and on the shore also leach nutrients directly into the groundwater, nutrients that can be absorbed by streamside plants. The relative role of this nutrient transfer versus that facilitated by bears depends on the topography, streambed type, proximity to the water, and the nature of the surrounding forest soils. In any case, bears depend upon salmon as an important food resource, which then subsidizes the fertilization of the forest, which in turn enriches the habitat of both salmon and bear, which is critical for the long-term survival of both.

o   o   o

CONSIDER THE Sitka deer *(Odocoileus hemionus sitkensi)*, a small-statured subspecies of mule deer that is closely related to the black-tailed deer found from California to Alaska. Sitka deer are found among the old-growth coastal rain forests of British Columbia and Alaska, particularly in the fall and winter months. Some deer are

year-round residents of the coastal forests, while others migrate to higher-altitude subalpine habitats in the summer. They are primary herbivores and browse on green-leafed shrubs and herbaceous vegetation like streamside and forest-understory grasses, salmonberry, bunchberry, and brambles that thrive in undisturbed areas. In the winter months, when much of the green foliage is under snow, they supplement their diet with lichens and browse from cedar and hemlock trees, without which the deer would starve. Access to this forest ecosystem is essential for their survival. In return, their feeding activity helps cycle marine-derived nutrients from streamside foliage to other trophic levels as they excrete nitrogenous wastes throughout their territory, even up into the mountains, and as they fall prey to bears and wolves. The nitrogen, carbon, and other elements that can be identified through

Capable swimmers when they need to be, Sitka deer *(Odocoileus hemionus sitkensi)* are a subspecies of mule deer that inhabit old-growth forests in British Columbia and Alaska. They are important grazers on the forest foliage and help cycle marine-derived nutrients through the Salmon Forest food web.

their stable isotopic signatures can be traced from the fertilizing excretions of the deer to the plants that they browse on, into the flesh of wolves that hunt the deer, back to the decomposing bodies of salmon and hence to the rich nutrient soup that fed the salmon during their years in the ocean.

It isn't just the magnitude of the pulse nutrients injected into the forest from a spawning run that is important, but also the timing, and therefore the effects of salmon on the ecosystem are complex and vary from place to place across the landscape. How the salmon bounty is transcribed into the terrestrial realm can differ even in watersheds located close to each other. The geomorphology of a high-latitude rocky mountain stream—the steepness, size, and composition of its bed, the nature of the surrounding soils, the steepness of its banks, and sinuousness of its course—can be different than that of a lower-latitude river or even a stream in a neighboring valley. The local climate and water temperature also affect salmon-forest interactions, and because a salmon population is strongly adapted and optimized to the conditions of its natal stream, the timing of spawning runs varies from one stream to another across the Pacific Northwest, even among subpopulations of the same salmon species. The complexities of the landscape then lead to great heterogeneity in the availability of salmon and salmon-derived marine nutrients over space and time. To a wide-ranging predator like a bear or a migratory bird traveling along the continent, a salmon feast is not restricted to a two- or three-week period; instead, predators and scavengers can gorge themselves over a much longer time, often months, by moving between different spawning populations. This extended feeding season is critical for certain migratory bird species that travel between the high Arctic and temperate and tropical regions and for animals, like bears, that must grow quickly during the typically short seasons of the north. The salmon's great capability to adapt to local conditions over a complex and varying continental landscape therefore has important resource implications for the entire Salmon Forest ecosystem, from the Arctic to the southern extent of its range, including Japan and the lower United States.

Researchers have recently discovered a wonderful example of the indirect role salmon play in the phenology of streamside flowering plants (phenology is the study of cycling and timing—which are often seasonally related—in biological systems). Adults of the blowfly (Calliphoridae spp.) are an important pollinator of many flowering plants, including kneeling angelica *(Angelica genuflexa)*, a common plant that grows one to two meters tall along many streams in the Pacific Northwest. The timing of its bloom coincides more closely to the timing of the spawning run of the stream next to which it resides than to more-typical plant-bloom-coordinating environmental cues, like temperature and length of daylight, that are conserved across many close watersheds. Kneeling angelica blooms approximately ten days after the spawning salmon start arriving at a particular stream. The spawning run leads to the accumulation of salmon carcasses along the stream; adult flies lay their eggs on the salmon carcasses, and the eggs then quickly grow into millions of carrion-eating maggot larvae. The maggots feast on salmon flesh and then pupate in the surrounding soil and emerge again the following season, precisely timed with the next salmon run. The hatched blowfly adults require nectar to grow and reproduce, which they harvest from streamside *A. genuflexa* that have their flowering precisely timed with the returning salmon. The blowfly adults and larvae feed upon the salmon bodies to energize their life cycle; and their activities ensure that the kneeling angelica is reliably pollinated year after year; and thus the salmon, even after death, support them all in synchrony.

T
O AN ECOLOGIST, organisms capable of profoundly modifying their habitat are known as ecosystem engineers, and ecosystem engineers are often identified as keystone species. The beaver *(Castor canadensis)* is an archetypal example; beavers transform streams into ponds by clearing foliage, felling trees, and damming the water flow. This activity radically alters their ecosystem, creating an entirely new habitat that is optimized for the niche of a beaver but also supports a diverse community of organisms different from that of the original drainage. Salmon too are consummate ecosystem engineers, so much so that it can be argued that their habitat-transforming efforts have evolved and shaped the coastal landscape over many thousands of square kilometers along the north Pacific rim.

Salmon work their transformative skills on both small and large environmental scales. When forming her redd, an adult female can disrupt more than a dozen square meters of streambed. By digging her nest into the bottom, she ensures that her eggs are protected from predators and potential scour from floodwaters. Her actions suspend fine sediment particles in the flowing water, and these are swept downstream from the nesting area. The streambed becomes a well-sorted substrate of clean, larger sand grains, pebbles, and cobbles much less susceptible to scour, and that increases interstitial water flow and oxygenation for the buried eggs and alevin. Over time, the combined actions of hundreds or thousands of spawning salmon can sift and shift tons of sediment in preferred nesting areas, forming flat gravel stretches and digging away at sand bars and channels and ultimately changing the course of the stream itself.

The churning of the streambed by nest digging also disturbs the community of organisms that use the surface of the substrate as their primary habitat. Salmon nesting buries benthic algae and aquatic insects or dislodges them to be swept downstream or consumed by other animals or both. Bottom coverage by benthic algae and populations of benthic invertebrates can decrease by 75 to 85 percent as a result of salmon nesting. However, these communities have adapted to withstand the regular disturbance associated with spawning, and they rebound very quickly by taking advantage of the pulse of nutrients injected into the stream by the decomposition of postspawning salmon carcasses. Some insects have evolved life cycles that are specifically synchronized with those of the salmon: they emerge or hatch as winged adults just before salmon spawning and so avoid the disruption of the sediment. Disturbance by biological forces, like bears rooting or salmon digging, and by abiotic forces, like fires or floods, is an important component shaping many ecosystems. Some systems are at their most productive and diverse when regularly perturbed by intermediate levels of disturbance. Low levels of disturbance allow some organisms to outcompete others and dominate a community; extreme levels of disturbance can cause entire communities to go extinct. At intermediate levels, there can be maximal community coexistence, which supports the greatest biodiversity. Species can evolve and adapt to regular disturbance like that created by the seasonal migration of spawning salmon—witness some plants that require fire to activate their seeds. Without disturbance, in conjunction with the ecological forces of predation and competition, the entire ecosystem is out of balance.

As the nutrients and energy released by postspawning salmon carcasses and carcass predation trickle into other trophic levels of the forest, ecosystem engineering on a broader scale is realized. The marine-derived nutrients exported from the stream subsidize the growth of the surrounding trees, shrubbery, and ground-covering plants. Spruce, cedar, hemlock, and willow trees that grow adjacent to a salmon stream show up to three times the normal growth rates, and the thickness and density of the high forest canopy increases with proximity to the stream. Large trees that are emblematic of old-growth forests provide a more diverse range of micro-habitats for colonization, from high canopy branches to the shaded forest floor, than do forests choked with predominantly dense tangles of brush, and also provide direct benefits to the salmon. Streams that are optimal provide habitat that is crucial for each stage of a salmon's life. Spawning adults, eggs, and alevin require clean, oxygenated waters with beds of well-sorted gravel and pebbles for nesting and early growth. Fry and parr require deeper waters, the space to hunt a diverse assemblage of food items, and protected areas that provide cover from predators. The improved growth rate of trees along salmon-running watersheds creates a powerful positive feedback mechanism that enhances the suitability of the drainage for salmon use. When towering old-growth trees collapse into streams or shed large woody debris, they create pools and logjams that provide exactly the right kind of habitat for salmon. These obstacles divert current flow, which then sculpts pools in the streambed, providing deep water for large salmon species and calm eddies in which juveniles can mature. Logjams also cause swift-running currents to dump their sediment load downstream of the dam, creating bars of gravel and sand and eventually forming islands and channels that braid the flow of water across river valleys and floodplains. And the woody debris barriers sieve the drifting carcasses of spent salmon from the rushing water, retaining them along the stream banks, where they decompose and provide the energy and nutrients to help cultivate the next stand of towering trees.

Plant growth in the Pacific Northwest is usually limited by the amount of nitrogen and phosphorus available in the soil, so a rich source of these essential nutrients stimulates growth. But, as with most things ecological, the exact relationship between the marine nutrients conveyed by the salmon to the coastal landscape and the autotrophic community is complex. The nutrients arrive in forms that are immediately both available and unavailable to plants. The enriched soil and groundwater can act as a nutrient storehouse before nitrogen and phosphorus and essential minerals are assimilated into the vegetation. And the decomposition of leaf litter and woody debris from the growing forest can both supplement the localized recycling of marine-derived nutrients and energy as well as dilute the marine-derived energy pathway with material generated from nonmarine sources. There is large variation in the amount of marine nutrient uptake into the forest, depending on the local geography (a steep, mountainous shoreline has a very different nutrient catchment than a coastal plain with a sinuous, gently flowing stream and estuary), the geology (some bedrock produces soils with a much higher concentration of phosphorus and other essential minerals), and the local plant species, not all of which are found across the entire Pacific Northwest. Proximity to the nutrient source is critical, and it follows that vegetation closest to a spawning stream produces foliage with the highest levels

Rotting on the bank of Pavlof Creek, Alaska, a salmon carcass is slowly consumed by a broad spectrum of carrion eaters. In a matter of weeks, all visible traces of the salmon will have been erased by the activities of small invertebrates and the stream and forest-floor microbial communities.

of marine-derived nitrogen and carbon, and that the nutrient influence is greatest within approximately 500 meters of the stream. Even with these caveats, the influence of salmon-transported nutrients and energy into terrestrial communities is enormous. The landscape of the Pacific Northwest is a mosaic of varying terrain types with an extensive network of estuaries, rivers, and streams forming watersheds west of the continental divide. Along the coast of British Columbia and southwest Alaska, over 90 percent of the forests can be found within five kilometers of what is or was once a salmon-bearing stream. And over this vast area, sometimes more than half the nitrogen nutrients cycling in the old-growth forests have come via the life cycle of the salmon. For the temperate rain forest in particular, this cycling and retention of nutrients is critical. Heavy rainfall tends to flush nutrients from thin soils; here, it is countered by the continuous influx of nutrients originally from the salmon and the buildup of decaying detritus from the long-lived trees.

The net effect of salmon on an ecosystem is formed from the balance between salmon being sources of enrichment and salmon being forces of disturbance, both roles complicated by the geomorphology of the landscape they live in. The same is true of nearly all creatures in the Salmon Forest and across the earth, including bears and eagles and native fishermen. Ecosystem dynamics in our world are rarely formulated with straightforward links that are easily defined and parameterized, or with a convenient separation between forces abiotic and biotic. Instead those dynamics are entwined under the guiding force of natural selection, linking hundreds of species in complex networks with often subtle feedback loops that provide hidden stability and that are difficult to ascertain. The salmon in the forest provides a unique window through which to observe the mechanisms that shape our planet.

Salmon modify their environment and at the same time evolve and adapt to it. This affects the degree of enrichment and disturbance brought by the salmon to the watershed. The grain size of sediments, the slope of the streambed, the residence time of the water—the physical attributes of the terrain—all play a role in regulating the effects of disturbance and nutrient input, which then regulate the degree to which marine-derived nutrients are

Old-growth alder, hemlock, and spruce trees draped in epiphytic moss and lichens shade the forest floor in the temperate rain forest of British Columbia. ▶

sequestered in the terrestrial environment. For example, the coarseness of the substrate found on the bottom of a spawning stream influences which salmon use it as a nesting site. The larger individuals are found in rivers with the coarsest particle sizes, because only they have the strength to carve their redds among the gravel and stones of the swiftest rivers, yet their nesting activities—their winnowing and digging—in turn influence the substrate that remains on the bottom.

It is important not to focus entirely on the nutrient energetics associated with the salmon's final acts of spawning and death. Although the net direction of nutrient flow is uphill from the marine communities into the forests via the salmon conveyor, there is also a lesser flow downstream. Spawning adults leave their large carcasses and nutrients upstream after death, but the eggs and smolts began their life cycle with an equally perilous downstream journey to the sea, with a concomitant transfer of nutrients to the ocean and the incorporation of this energy into marine food webs. Eggs and smolts are comparatively small, but they being life's journey in numbers far greater than the number of spawning adults. Their mortality is high, and collectively, predation on the young life history stages of the salmon is an important energetic component in marine food webs.

Some studies have shown that one of the most important factors controlling the overall productivity of a stream isn't the number of carcasses that litter the banks after spawning, but the number of live salmon that begin the run. The carcass of a salmon after spawning is a ghostly shell of watery tissue, nearly all the cellular energy having been consumed by the metabolic demands of procreation. It carries just a fraction of the nutrients and vitality of a robust, recently matured adult, which eats and excretes and gets eaten and forms an important component in both marine and terrestrial ecosystems. In fact, we now realize that dumping fish carcasses into watersheds that used to support thriving salmon populations in an attempt to duplicate the seasonal introduction of salmon-derived marine nutrients from spawning runs unfortunately does not provide nearly the productivity boost to the system one might expect. The presence of dead salmon, even in large numbers, does not replicate the complex interactions that a live and thriving population brings to the Salmon Forest.

In the tenth century, on the island of Shikoku in southeastern Japan, fishermen sensed a connection between the state of their nearshore fishery and the quality of their coastal forests. The critical habitat was named *Uotsuki-rin,* the "fish-breeding forest," a concept reinforced by the ruling shogun. By the time of the Tokugawa period, from 1603 to 1868, it had developed into a relatively advanced forest management policy, and protected *Uotsuki-rin* could be found throughout Japan. A policy forbidding the cutting of trees and clearing of land in certain regions was an effort to maintain local stocks of anadromous fishes—*masu* and *yamame*—and most important, to protect offshore populations of herring and sardine, which were fished not only for food but to provide fish-based fertilizer for rice cultivation. In 1897 the new Meiji government codified the First Forest Law governing the "fish-breeding forest" in order to protect fisheries' resources. The *Uotsuki-rin* provided shade to shield streams and rivers from excessive heat, furnished protective cover for fish, protected banks from erosion and runoff, and aided stream productivity through leaf fall and dissolved nutrients. It wasn't until more recently that the importance of the natural marine-nutrient conveyor created by the return of anadromous fishes, like the salmon, was truly appreciated and the *Uotsuki-rin* were seen as self-perpetuating. Instead the conceptual emphasis was on the *Uotsuki-rin* primarily

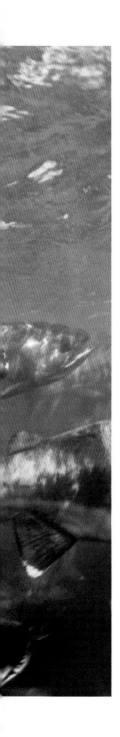

benefiting the oceanic ecosystems, despite the activities of farmers fertilizing the land with fish meal, in a role akin to that of a bear.

There was prescience in *Animal Farm*'s bastardized seventh commandment, "All animals are equal, but some animals are more equal than others." George Orwell's dystopian allegory notwithstanding, keystone species interactions, like those between the salmon and the bear, are more important than those between other organisms; they profoundly influence the entire ecosystem. Without the salmon and the bear, the forests of the Pacific Northwest would not be the same, and the coastal landscape of the entire region could be very different.

Imagine a world without salmon: not just a world where they thrived and then were driven to extinction, but a world where they never evolved, a world where *Eosalmo* never swam in the lakes at Driftwood Canyon and where rivers never turned into bright scarlet gashes choked with the backs of migrating sockeye. The Pacific Northwest forests in this imaginary world wouldn't support the current number of predators that rely on salmon spawning. There would be fewer bears and gulls and eagles, certainly not the large aggregations that cluster near nesting streams. There would be fewer fish that feed on salmon eggs or smolt, fewer marine mammals that feed on adults in the sea, and certainly none of the organisms that evolve in tight lockstep with the salmon, like their parasites and viruses. There would be fewer nutrients carried far into the interior by migrating animals that feed in the forest. And because the presence of the salmon extends beyond those organisms that touch its flesh directly, the salmon bounty wouldn't extend into all the indirect interactions that shape the ecosystem and landscape. There would be fewer deer browsing streambank grasses, and fewer wolves to hunt them. Without the presence of salmon carcasses, trees wouldn't grow as fast or as thick along the streams. The nearby forests could become choked with low-diversity brush because there would be fewer bears digging and rooting about in the soil. In the absence of a lush forest root system, rushing rain could wash away topsoil on higher slopes. Stream bottoms could become silt laden and stagnant without the salmon's tireless digging of nests. Less old-growth debris would fall and clog the rivers, meaning fewer deep pools for other fishes. This world without salmon also wouldn't have the rich indigenous cultures that settled around the Pacific rim to take advantage of the lushness of the landscape nurtured by the fish in the forest.

Nature is nothing if not full of surprises, and natural selection is a powerful force. Perhaps the niche of the salmon would be immediately filled by a substitute fish, one that would evolve in tight synchrony with the changing landscape. There are other fishes across the world that possess the unique characteristics of semelparity and anadromy; some even swim alongside the salmon. There are candlefish, smelt, and shad that swim the Pacific and then enter freshwater to spawn. They are important fishes in their own way, but they haven't capitalized on the freshwater habitat to the same degree as the salmon, and not all of them show the salmon's tight homing instinct. There are sturgeon, which reach a huge size and enter estuaries and large swift rivers to spawn but which spend most of their lives in the sea and don't perish after spawning, delivering their nutrient-laden bodies to the forest. And there are other anadromous salmonids, like coastal-living brown, cutthroat, and rainbow trout, which also transfer important marine nutrients into terrestrial ecosystems, but to a much lesser degree than those species of Pacific salmon, whose massive migrations can dominate a watershed. Perhaps one of these or a related species would evolve and adapt to a world without salmon and take their place. It is most interesting that there are no salmon surrogates in the southern hemisphere, where one would think similar niches would be available for exploitation. No salmon or salmon-like fishes naturally swarm the streams and rivers of South America, Australia, or New Zealand to spawn and die and enrich the land. Only now, after we have artificially introduced them to these regions and observed them flourish, outcompete other fishes, and extend their range, can we see that perhaps those empty niche spaces might never have been filled at all, and that a world without salmon would remain forever exactly that.

o   o   o

THERE IS a rich mythology among the First Nation tribes of the Pacific Northwest that illustrates their deep connection not just with the salmon, but with the complex ecosystem that is the Salmon Forest. Whether from Haida, Tlingit, Chinook, or the great number of other native peoples, their stories of creation and metaphors for life are deeply interwoven within a culture that persisted because of an understanding of the fragile connection between man, the salmon, and the inhabitants of the forest. Without the salmon and the benefit of a dependable source of food that could be preserved to last a long winter in the north, it is probably fair to say that their advanced societies might never have developed. And still, lean salmon years often meant starvation.

To the Kwakwaka'wakw of British Columbia, the "Salmon People" live in human guise in a village far beneath the sea and over the ocean horizon to the west. It is a parallel world of immortal children, women, and men who go about their lives much the same as their terrestrial counterparts. Each year the Salmon People migrate to their spawning grounds and so must take on their scaled form, as "the swimmers," to complete their journey. The waiting native fishermen welcome them back to the world of men as supernatural beings and honor them as the bringers of life to their community. The swimmers' flesh is smoked and dried, but their bones are returned to the rivers where the currents and the tides carry them back out to the ocean. There they regain their flesh and blood and live again as the Salmon People in the village beneath the sea—parallel lives in connected parallel worlds.

The Salmon People mythology instills an ethos that is found among nearly all the native cultures that were established within the watersheds of the great spawning runs, and although the exact expression varies from tribe to tribe, there is a universal admiration for the beauty and value of this special fish. In a story that pervades the region, there was once a hungry young boy who was disrespectful of his mother and her proffered salmon meal. Refusing to eat, he went to play and swim in the river. There, swift currents dragged him away from his friends and he was swept far out to sea, where he was pulled below the waves and drowned. The Salmon People caught his drowning soul and carried it with them back to their village beneath the sea, and the young boy lived on in this parallel spirit world. The Salmon People raised him as their own and taught him that if he was hungry, he should go to a stream and catch one of the Salmon children swimming there, but he should be sure to return the bones and whatever was left back to the stream, so that the Salmon child could come back to life. When it was time, the boy swam with the Salmon People back to

The monumental carvings and totem poles made by the First Nation peoples of the Pacific Northwest stand as complex artistic and cultural symbols illustrating legends, tribal history, or important local events. Representation of key animals in the carvings, like bears and salmon, indicate the importance of these creatures in the mythology and sociology of native cultures. ▶

the rivers in the world of men, where he was caught by his mother. She could recognize his soul in the beautiful fish, so she carefully protected him and nurtured him, and he shed his salmon skin and became human once again. The boy became a powerful shaman for his tribe and taught the tribal members the ways to respect the Salmon People. One day a large salmon carcass came floating downstream after the spawning migration, and the shaman recognized it as harboring his soul. When he speared it, his mortal body died again, and the people of his village placed his body back into the river, where it drifted back to sea and sank again to the home of the Salmon People. To this day, salmon are respected and elaborate ceremonies are performed with the capture of the first fish of the season. They are treated reverentially and their bones are returned to the rivers to ensure that other spawning salmon will follow.

The story of the salmon in myth and in science is one of transformation and eternal regeneration, death, sacrifice, and resurrection. The "King of Fish" is an admirable choice for a divine creature of legend because of its incredible strength, endurance, and life-sustaining importance. As salmon develop, their bodies undergo radical metamorphosis both externally and in their adapting, internal physiology. They hatch in freshwater pools, disappear into the ocean, and then return to spawn and die en masse. Their bodies feed the forest and their progeny fill the streams again in a cycle that is as close to a resurrection as there ever could be.

Many thousands of different animals and plants make up the Salmon Forest ecosystem. When you include hillside forests, grasslands, coastal estuaries, and offshore seas, places far removed from the streams where salmon spawn but are nonetheless important to the life history of the salmon, the number of species linked to the Salmon Forest becomes overwhelming. It becomes very difficult to define the boundaries, the potential niche space, of the salmon. Oceanic nutrients transported upstream by salmon on their final swim find their way through a multitude of trophic linkages and are detectable in communities thousands of kilometers from the sea. If we consider the importance of the salmon spawning bounty to a host of wide-ranging migrants like far-flying terns and gulls, an ever more delicate and expanding web of connections branches outward from the Salmon Forest to encompass the entire continent.

It has been calculated that before the development of the major commercial salmon fisheries, spawning salmon transported almost 7,000 tons of elemental nitrogen and 1,000 tons of phosphorus to the coastal forest ecosystem each year. If all the salmon caught in the early 1900s were miraculously returned to the forest, the nutrients from their bodies alone would support more than 200,000 tons of additional plant growth, countless hectares of foliage, or more than 5,000 large old-growth cedar trees. At the turn of the twentieth century, approximately 45 million salmon migrated each year into watersheds from California to Washington. At the beginning of the twenty-first century, the torrent of returning salmon has mostly ceased in these southerly regions, due to anthropogenic impacts. Only about 2 million salmon now return, providing less than 20 percent of the original biomass and nutrient input to those rivers and streams that still support spawning, and no nutrient subsidy at all to over 40 percent of their original landscape range—places where they have now gone extinct. In Canada and Alaska, there are still streams that run thick with spawning salmon; however, there too, populations are in decline due to fishing pressure and habitat disruption. The decline is a double-edged sword: fewer fish return, providing less energy and nutrients to the forest, which supports the next generation.

Already capable of incredible strength and leaping ability, young salmon in an Alaskan hatchery attempt to jump their way up the powerful rush of freshwater coming from a discharge pipe.

o　o　o

HOW MUCH is a salmon worth? We typically view salmon as a commodity, and we price them by the kilogram of their dead flesh, a sad reflection on how difficult or easy they might be to catch and how eager we are to eat them. We don't appraise their worth by including their overarching benefit to the environment—as an essential part of a miraculous conveyor of nutrients and energy from the land to the sea and back again, and as a key species in a web of trophic interactions that includes hundreds, if not thousands, of other species. It becomes difficult to know when to stop calculating the benefits and value of a creature, atoms of which can be traced from the ocean to treetops far removed from any shore. If we truly valued the intrinsic worth of a salmon as a part of the Salmon Forest, perhaps we'd realize that we can't afford to exploit them—and we wouldn't want to.

Species of *Oncorhynchus* have proven to be resilient fish. In the 50 million years since the first *Eosalmo* swam in freshwater lakes, and in the 15,000 years since the withdrawal of the continental ice sheets, salmon have inhabited and coevolved with the forests of the Pacific Northwest. Their combined characteristics of anadromy, semelparity, and natal homing reinforce evolutionary adaptation to their environment, from single streams to ocean basins, and from generations to thousands of years. Evolving in synchrony with the landscape has made them consummate survivors and helped shape the very structure of the land around them.

Stories of sacrifice, death, and resurrection are pervasive across all cultures. Among the First Nation peoples of the Pacific Northwest, such stories are commensurate with a culture dependent not only on a fish but on the landscape they share. To the modern cohabitants of the Pacific north who are of Christian faith, sacrifice, death, and resurrection are summarized in the act of reparation instilled within the Via Crucis, the Way of the Cross, and the subsequent resurrection of Christ. As interpreted by the First Nation People of the Salmon Forest, the salmon too followed a similar path—of struggle and hardship, death, and then a generation reborn and an environment enriched. Perhaps it is fitting that the Via Crucis was established by St. Francis of Assisi, the patron saint of animals and the environment. In his Canticle of All Creatures, St. Francis exults, "Praised be You, my Lord, through our Sister Mother Earth, who sustains and governs us," and we are urged to find wonder and glory in all the creatures of earth. The story of the Salmon Forest begins and ends with a fish. As we are the keepers of the salmon, and the forest, our true moral test will be whether the story will continue or whether it will be lost, and then, as in the Way of the Cross, we will find ourselves performing acts of atonement.

ACKNOWLEDGMENTS

WE WOULD LIKE TO THANK esteemed ichthyologists John McCosker, Dr. Leighton Taylor, and Dr. Richard Rosenblatt for their friendly advice and critical commentary. We would also like to thank Eric Prestegard at DIPAC Macaulay fish hatchery in Juneau and Erin Hunt at the California Wolf Center in Julian for being so generous with their time and resources. We thank Shad Bee, Josh Yerkes, and Derek Kyostia for their assistance in and out of the field. Doc White also thanks friends Kevin Finan, Scott Launey, and Jim Shine for their help, and especially his wife, Ceci White, for her tireless support as able assistant, safety diver, boat driver, and model. Finally, we thank the wonderful people of British Columbia and Alaska, who could always be counted on to share their beautiful landscape.

Adams, L., S. Farley, C. Stricker, D. Demma, G. Roffler, D. Miller, R. Rye. 2010. Are inland wolf-ungulate systems influenced by marine subsidies of Pacific salmon? Ecological Applications 20: 251–262.

Allee, W., A. Emerson, O. Park, T. Park, K. Schmidt. 1949. Principles of animal ecology. Philadelphia: Saunders.

Armstrong, J., D. Schindler, K. Omori, C. Ruff, T. Quinn. 2010. Thermal heterogeneity mediates the effects of pulsed subsidies across a landscape. Ecology 91: 1445–1454.

Au, W., J. Ford, J. Horne, K. Newman Allman. 2004. Echolocation of free-ranging killer whales *(Orcinus orca)* and modeling of foraging for chinook salmon *(Oncorhynchus tshawytscha)*. J. Acoust. Soc. Am. 115: 901–909.

Au, W., J. Horne, C. Jones. 2010. Basis of acoustic discrimination of chinook salmon from other salmons by echolocating *Orcinus orca*. J. Acoust. Soc. Am. 128: 2225–2232.

Bartz, K., R. Naiman. 2005. Effects of salmon-borne nutrients on riparian soils and vegetation in southwest Alaska. Ecosystems 8: 529–545.

Beamish, R., C. Mahnken. 2001. A critical size and period hypothesis to explain natural regulation of salmon abundance and the linkage to climate and climate change. Progress in Oceanography 49: 423–437.

Beamish, R., G. McFarlane, J. King. 2005. Migratory patterns of pelagic fishes and possible linkages between open ocean and coastal ecosystems off the Pacific coast of North America. Deep Sea Research II 52: 739–755.

Ben-David, M., T. Hanley, D. Klein, D. Schell. 1997. Seasonal changes in diets of coastal and riverine mink: The role of spawning Pacific salmon. Can. J. Zool. 75: 803–811.

Ben-David, M., T. Hanley, D. Schell. 1998. Fertilization of terrestrial vegetation by spawning Pacific salmon: The role of flooding and predator activity. Oikos 83: 47–55.

Ben-David, M., K. Titus, L. Beier. 2004. Consumption of salmon by Alaskan brown bears: A trade-off between nutritional requirements and the risk of infanticide? Oecologia 138: 465–474.

Bennetts, R., B. McClelland. 1997. Influence of age and prey availability on bald eagle foraging behavior at Glacier National Park, Montana. Wilson Bull. 109: 393–409.

Bilby, R., E. Beach, B. Fransen, J. Walter. 2003. Transfer of nutrients from spawning salmon to riparian vegetation in western Washington. Trans. Am. Fish. Soc. 132: 733–745.

Bilby, R., B. Fransen, P. Bisson. 1996. Incorporation of nitrogen and carbon from spawning coho salmon into the trophic system of small streams: Evidence from stable isotopes. Can. J. Fish. Aquat. Sci. 53: 164–173.

Candy, J., T. Beacham. 2000. Patterns of homing and straying in southern British Columbia coded-wire tagged chinook salmon *(Oncorhynchus tshawytscha)* populations. Fisheries Res. 47: 41–56.

Carlson, S., T. Quinn, A. Hendry. 2011. Eco-evolutionary dynamics in Pacific salmon. Heredity 10.1038/hdy.2010.163.

Carlson, S., H. Rich, T. Quinn. 2009. Does variation in selection imposed by bears drive divergence among populations in the size and shape of sockeye salmon? Evolution 63: 1244–1261.

Cederholm, C., M. Kunze, T. Murota, A. Sibatani. Pacific salmon carcasses: Essential contributions of nutrients and energy for aquatic and terrestrial ecosystems. Fisheries 24: 6–15.

Chaloner, D., K. Martin, M. Wipfli, P. Ostrom, G. Lamberti. 2002. Marine carbon and nitrogen in southeastern Alaska stream food webs: Evidence from artificial and natural streams. Can. J. Fish. Aquat. Sci. 59: 1257–1265.

Chaloner, D., M. Wipfli. 2002. Influence of decomposing Pacific salmon carcasses on macroinvertebrate growth and standing stock in southeastern Alaska streams. J. N. Am. Bentho. Soc. 21: 430–442.

Chaloner, D., M. Wipfli, J. Caouette. 2002. Mass loss and macroinvertebrate colonization of Pacific salmon carcasses in south-eastern
  Alaska streams. Freshwater Biology 47: 263–273.

Christie, K., M. Hocking, T. Reimchen. 2008. Tracing salmon nutrients
  in riparian food webs: Isotopic evidence in a ground-foraging passerine. Can. J. Zool. 86: 1317–1323.

Christie, K., T. Reimchen. 2005. Post-reproductive Pacific salmon, *Oncorhynchus* spp., as a major nutrient source for large aggregations
  of gulls, *Larus* spp. Canadian Field Naturalist 119: 202–207.

Darimont, C., T. Reimchen. 2002. Intra-hair stable isotope analysis implies seasonal shift to salmon in gray wolf diet. Can. J. Zool. 80:
  1638–1642.

Darimont, C., T. Reimchen, P. Paquet. 2003. Foraging behavior by gray
  wolves on salmon streams in coastal British Columbia. Can. J.
  Zool. 81: 349–353.

Dittman, A., T. Quinn. 1996. Homing in Pacific salmon: Mechanisms
  and ecological basis. J. Experimental Biology 199: 83–91.

Doucett, R., G. Power, D. Barton, R. Drimmie, R. Cunjak. 1996. Stable
  isotope analysis of nutrient pathways leading to Atlantic salmon.
  Can. J. Fish. Aquat. Sci. 53: 2058–2066.

Drake, D., R. Naiman, J. Helfield. 2002. Reconstructing salmon abundance in rivers: An initial dendrochronological evaluation. Ecology 83: 2971–2977.

Edmonds, R., K. Mikkelsen. 2006. Influence of salmon carcass place-
  ment in red alder riparian areas on stream chemistry in lowland
  western Washington. N. Am. J. Fish. Manag. 26: 551–558.

Evenden, M. 2004. Social and environmental change at Hells Gate,
  British Columbia. J. Historical Geography 30: 130–153.

Fausch, K., M. Power, M. Murakami. 2002. Linkages between stream
  and forest food webs: Shigeru Nakano's legacy for ecology in Japan. Trends in Ecology and Evolution 17: 0169–5347/02.

Finney, B., I. Gregory-Eaves, J. Sweetman, M. Douglas, J. Smol. 2000.
  Impacts of climatic change and fishing on Pacific salmon abundance over the past 300 years. Science 290: 795–799.

Ford, J., G. Ellis. 2006. Selective foraging by fish-eating killer whales
  Orcinus orca in British Columbia. Mar. Ecol. Prog. Ser. 316: 185–
  199.

Ford, J., G. Ellis, L. Barrett-Lennard, A. Morton, R. Palm, K. Balcomb. 1998. Dietary specialization in two sympatric populations of killer whales *(Orcinus orca)* in coastal British Columbia and adjacent waters. Can. J. Zool. 76: 1456–1471.

Francis, T., D. Schindler, J. Moore. 2006. Aquatic insects play a minor role in dispersing salmon-derived nutrients into riparian forests in southwestern Alaska. Can. J. Fish. Aquat. Sci. 63: 2543–2552.

Gende, S., R. Edwards, M. Willson, M. Wipfli. 2002. Pacific salmon in aquatic and terrestrial ecosystems. BioScience 52: 917–928.

Gende, S., M. Willson. 2001. Passerine densities in riparian forests of southeast Alaska: Potential effects of anadromous spawning salmon. Condor 103: 624–629.

Gould, J. 2008. Animal navigation: The evolution of magnetic orientation. Current Biology 18: R482.

Greist, D., D. Dauble. 1998. Redd site selection and spawning habitat use by fall chinook salmon: The importance of geomorphic features in large rivers. Environmental Management 22: 655–669.

Groot, G., L. Margolis (eds). 1991. Pacific salmon: Life histories. Seattle: University of Washington Press.

Gross, M., R. Coleman, R. McDowall. 1988. Aquatic productivity and the evolution of diadromous fish migration. Science 239: 1291–1293.

Gunther, E. 1926. An analysis of the first salmon ceremony. American Anthropologist 28: 605–617.

Hamon, T., C. Foote, G. Brown. 1999. Use of female nest characteristics in the sexual behavior of male sockeye salmon. J. Fish Biol. 55:459–471.

Hanson, A. 1987. Regulation of bald eagle reproductive rates in southeast Alaska. Ecology 68: 1387–1392.

Hauser, D., M. Logsdon, E. Holmes, G. VanBlaricom, R. Osborne. 2007. Summer distribution patterns of southern resident killer whales *Orcinus orca:* Core areas and spatial aggregation of social groups. Mar. Ecol. Prog. Ser. 351: 301–310.

Heimlich-Boran, J. 1988. Behavioral ecology of killer whales *(Orcinus orca)* in the Pacific Northwest. Can. J. Zool. 66: 546–578.

Helfield, J., R. Naiman. 2001. Effects of salmon-derived nitrogen on riparian forest growth and implications for stream productivity. Ecology 82: 2403–2409.

———. 2002. Salmon and alder as nitrogen sources to riparian forest in a boreal Alaskan watershed. Oecologia 133: 573–582.

———. 2006. Keystone interactions: Salmon and bear in riparian forests of Alaska. Ecosystems 9: 167–180.

Herman, D., D. Burrow, P. Wade, J. Durban, C. Matkin, R. LeDuc, L. Barrett-Lennard, M. Krahn. 2005. Feeding ecology of eastern north Pacific killer whales *Orcinus orca* from fatty acid, stable isotope, and organochlorine analyses of blubber biopsies. Mar. Ecol. Prog. Ser. 302: 275–291.

Hicks, B., M. Wipfli, D. Lang, M. Lang. 2005. Marine-derived nitrogen and carbon in freshwater-riparian food webs of the Copper River delta, southcentral Alaska. Oecologia 144: 558–569.

Hilderbrand, G., T. Hanley, C. Robbins, C. Schwartz. 1999. Role of brown bears *(Ursus arctos)* in the flow of marine nitrogen into a terrestrial ecosystem. Oecologia 121: 546–550.

Hoar, W., D. Randall (eds). 1969. Fish physiology. Volume 1. Excretion, ionic regulation, and metabolism. New York: Academic Press.

Hobson, K. 1999. Tracing origins and migration of wildlife using stable isotopes: A review. Oecologia 120: 314–326.

Hocking, M., C. Darimont, K. Christie, T. Reimchen. 2007. Niche variation in burying beetles (*Nicrophorus* spp.) associated with marine and terrestrial carbon. Can. J. Zool. 85: 437–442.

Hocking, M., T. Reimchen. 2002. Salmon-derived nitrogen in terrestrial invertebrates from coniferous forests of the Pacific Northwest. BMC Ecology 2:4/1472-6785/2/4.

———. 2006. Consumption and distribution of salmon (*Oncorhynchus* spp.) nutrients and energy by terrestrial flies. Can. J. Fish. Aquat. Sci. 63: 2076–2086.

Hocking, M., D. Reynolds. 2012. Nitrogen uptake by plants subsidized by Pacific salmon carcasses: A hierarchical experiment. Can. J. For. Res. 42: 908–917.

Hocking, M., R. Ring, T. Reimchen. 2006. Burying beetle *Nicrophorus investigator* reproduction on Pacific salmon carcasses. Ecological Entomology 31: 5–12.

———. 2009. The ecology of terrestrial invertebrates on Pacific salmon carcasses. Ecol. Res. 24: 1091–1100.

Holtgrieve, G., D. Schindler. 2011. Marine-derived nutrients, bioturbation, and ecosystem metabolism: Reconsidering the role of salmon in streams. Ecology 92: 373–385.

Holtgrieve, G., D. Schindler, C. Gowell, C. Ruff, P. Lisi. 2010. Stream geomorphology regulates the effects on periphyton of ecosystem engineering and nutrient enrichment by Pacific salmon. Freshwater Biology 55: 2598–2611.

Hutchinson, G. 1959. Homage to Santa Rosalia or why are there so many kinds of animals? American Naturalist 93: 145–159.

———. 1961. The paradox of the plankton. American Naturalist 95: 137–145.

Janetski, D., D. Chaloner, S. Tiegs, G. Lamberti. 2009. Pacific salmon effects on stream ecosystems: A quantitative synthesis. Oecologia 159: 583–595.

Jonsson, B., N. Jonsson. 2003. Migratory Atlantic salmon as vectors for the transfer of energy and nutrients between freshwater and marine environments. Freshwater Biology 48: 21–27.

Kirschvink, J., M. Walker, S.-B. Chang, A. Dizon, K. Peterson. 1985. Chains of single-domain magnetite particles in chinook salmon, *Oncorhynchus tshawytscha*. J. Comp. Physio. A. 157: 375–381.

Kline, T., J. Goering, O. Mathisen, P. Poe, P. Parker. 1990. Recycling of elements transported upstream of runs of Pacific salmon: $\delta^{15}N$ and $\delta^{13}C$ evidence in Sashin Creek, southeastern Alaska. Can. J. Aquat. Sci. 47: 136–144.

Koyama, A., K. Kavanagh, A. Robinson. 2005. Marine nitrogen in central Idaho riparian forests: Evidence from stable isotopes. Can. J. Fish. Aquat. Sci. 62: 518–526.

Kroes, H. 1997. The niche structure of ecosystems. J. Theor. Biol. 65: 317–326.

Lantis, M. 1938. The mythology of Kodiak Island, Alaska. Journal of American Folklore 51: 9–172.

Lema, S., G. Nevitt. 2004. Evidence that thyroid hormone induces olfactory cellular proliferations in salmon during a sensitive period for imprinting. J. Experimental Biol. 207: 3317–3327.

Lessard, J., R. Merritt, M. Berg. 2009. Investigating the effect of marine-derived nutrients from spawning salmon on macroinvertebrate secondary production in southeast Alaskan streams. J. N. Am. Benthol. Soc. 28: 683–693.

Levi, P., J. Tank, S. Tiegs, J. Ruegg, D. Chaloner, G. Lamberti. 2011. Does timber harvest influence the dynamics of marine-derived nutrients in southeast Alaska streams? Can. J. Fish. Aquat. Sci. 68: 1316–1329.

Levi, T., C. Darimont, M. MacDuffee, M. Mangel, P. Paquet, C. Wilmers.

2012. Using grizzly bears to assess harvest-ecosystem trade-offs in salmon fisheries. PLoS Biol 10(4): e1001303. doi:10.1371/journal.pbio.1001303.

Lisi, P., D. Schindler. 2011. Spatial variation in timing of marine subsidies influences riparian phenology through a plant-pollinator mutualism. Ecosphere 2: 1–14.

Lohmann, K., N. Putman, C. Lohmann. 2008. Geomagnetic imprinting: A unifying hypothesis of long-distance natal homing in salmon and sea turtles. PNAS 105: 19096–19101.

Mathewson, D., M. Hocking, T. Reimchen. 2003. Nitrogen uptake in riparian plant communities across a sharp ecological boundary of salmon density. BMC Ecology 3:4/1472–6785/3/4.

McDowall, R. 2001a. Anadromy and homing: Two life-history traits with adaptive synergies in salmonid fishes? Fish and Fisheries 2: 78–85.

———. 2001b. Diadromy, diversity and divergence: Implications for speciation processes in fishes. Fish and Fisheries 2: 278–285.

———. 2002. The origin of the salmonid fishes: Marine, freshwater . . . or neither? Reviews in Fish Biology and Fisheries 11: 171–179.

———. 2008. Why are so many boreal freshwater fishes anadromous? Confronting conventional wisdom. Fish and Fisheries 9: 208–213.

McPhee, M., T. Quinn. 1998. Factors affecting the duration of next defense and reproductive lifespan of female sockeye salmon, *Oncorhynchus nerka*. Environ. Biology of Fishes 51: 369–375.

Merz, J., P. Moyle. 2006. Salmon, wildlife and wine: Marine-derived nutrients in human-dominated ecosystems of central California. Ecological Applications 16: 999–1009.

Minikawa, N., R. Gara. 2005. Spatial and temporal distribution of coho salmon carcasses in a stream in the Pacific Northwest, USA. Hydrobiologia 539: 163–166.

Minikawa, N., R. Gara, J. Honea. 2002. Increased individual growth rate and community biomass of stream insects associated with salmon carcasses. J. N. Am. Benth. Soc. 21: 651–659.

Mobrand, L., J. Lichatowich, L. Lestelle, T. Vogel. 1997. An approach to describing ecosystem performance "through the eyes of a salmon." Can. J. Fish. Aquat. Sci. 54: 2964–2973.

Montgomery, D. 2003. King of fish: The thousand-year run of salmon. Boulder, CO: Westview.

Moore, J., S. Hayes, W. Duffy, S. Gallagher, C. Michel, D. Wright. 2011. Nutrient fluxes and the recent collapse of coastal California salmon populations. Can. J. Fish. Aquat. Sci. 68: 1161–1170.

Moore, J., D. Schindler. 2007. Biotic disturbance and benthic community dynamics in salmon-bearing streams. J. Animal Ecol. 77: 275–284.

Moore, J., D. Schindler, J. Carter, J. Fox, J. Griffiths, G. Holtgrieve. 2007. Biotic control of stream fluxes: Spawning salmon drive nutrient and matter export. Ecology 88: 1278–1291.

Moore, J., D. Schindler, M. Scheuerell. 2004. Disturbance of freshwater habitats by anadromous salmon in Alaska. Oecologia 139: 298–308.

Naiman, R., R. Bilby, P. Bisson. 2000. Riparian ecology and management in the Pacific coastal rain forest. BioScience 50: 996–1011.

Naiman, R., R. Bilby, D. Schindler, J. Helfield. 2002. Pacific salmon, nutrients and the dynamics of freshwater and riparian ecosystems. Ecosystems 5: 399–417.

Nakano, S., M. Murakami. 2001. Reciprocal subsidies: Dynamic interdependence between terrestrial and aquatic food webs. PNAS 98: 166–170.

Nelson, J. 1984. Fishes of the world. New York: Wiley.

Nichol, L., D. Shackelton. 1996. Seasonal movements and foraging behavior of northern resident killer whales *(Orcinus orca)* in relation to the inshore distribution of salmon (*Oncorhynchus* spp.) in British Columbia. Can. J. Zool. 74: 983–991.

Paine, R. 1969a. A note on trophic complexity and community stability. American Naturalist 103: 91–93.

———. 1969b. The Pisaster-Tegula interaction: Prey patches, predator food preference, and intertidal community structure. Ecology 50: 950–961.

Pess, G., D. Montgomery, E. Steel, R. Bilby, B. Feist, H. Greenberg. 2002. Landscape characteristics, land use, and coho salmon *(Oncorhynchus kisutch)* abundance, Snohomish River, Wash., USA. Can. J. Fish. Aquat. Sci. 59: 613–623.

Power, M., D. Tilman, J. Estes, B. Menge, W. Bond, L. Mills, G. Daily, J. Castilla, J. Lubchenco, R. Paine. 1996. Challenges in the quest for keystones. BioScience 46: 609–620.

Quinn, T. 1991. Models of Pacific salmon orientation and navigation on the open ocean. J. Theor. Biol. 150: 539–545.

———. 2005. The behavior and ecology of Pacific salmon and trout. Seattle: University of Washington Press.

Quinn, T., G. Buck. 2001. Size- and sex-selective mortality of adult sockeye salmon: Bears, gulls, and fish out of water. Trans. Am. Fish. Soc. 130: 995–1005.

Reimchen, T. 2000. Some ecological and evolutionary aspects of bear-salmon interactions in coastal British Columbia. Can. J. Zool. 78: 448–457.

———. 2001. Salmon nutrients, nitrogen isotopes and coastal forests. Ecoforestry 2001: 13–16.

Reimchen, T., D. Mathewson, M. Hocking, J. Moran, D. Harris. 2002. Isotopic evidence for enrichment of salmon-derived nutrients in vegetation, soil, and insects in riparian zones in coastal British Columbia. American Fisheries Society Symposium 2002: 1–10.

Ruegg, J., D. Chaloner, P. Levi, J. Tank, S. Tiegs, G. Lamberti. 2012. Environmental variability and the ecological effects of spawning Pacific salmon on stream biofilm. Freshwater Ecology 57: 129–142.

Sapir, E. 1907. Preliminary report on the language and mythology of the upper Chinook. American Anthropologist 9: 533–544.

Satterfield, F., B. Finney. 2002. Stable isotope analysis of Pacific salmon: Insight into trophic status and oceanographic conditions of the last 30 years. Progress in Oceanography 53: 231–246.

Saulitis, E., C. Matkin, L. Barrett-Lennard, K. Heise, G. Ellis. 2000. Foraging strategies of sympatric killer whale *(Orcinus orca)* populations in Prince William Sound, Alaska. Marine Mammal Sci. 16: 94–109.

Schindler, D., M. Scheuerell, J. Moore, S. Gende, T. Francis. 2003. Pacific salmon and the ecology of coastal ecosystems. Front. Ecol. Environ. 1: 31–37.

Schlosser, I. 1991. Stream fish ecology: A landscape perspective. BioScience 41: 704–712.

Spencer, C., B. McClelland, J. Stanford. 1991. Shrimp stocking, salmon collapse, and eagle displacement. BioScience 41: 14–21.

Stalmaster, M., J. Gessaman. 1984. Ecological energetics and foraging behavior of overwintering bald eagles. Ecological Monographs 54: 407–428.

Stalmaster, M., J. Newman, A. Hansen. 1979. Population dynamics of wintering bald eagles on the Nooksack River, Washington. Northwest Science 53: 126–131.

Stouder, D., P. Bisson, R. Naiman (eds). 1996. Pacific salmon and their ecosystems. New York: Chapman and Hall.

Szepanski, M., M. Ben-David, V. Van Ballenberghe. 1999. Assessment of anadromous salmon resources in the diet of the Alexander Archipelago wolf using stable isotope analysis. Oecologia 120: 327–335.

Taylor, E. 1991. A review of local adaptation in Salmonidae, with particular reference to Pacific and Atlantic salmon. Aquaculture 98: 185–207.

Taylor, E., C. Foote, C. Wood. 1996. Molecular genetic evidence for parallel life-history evolution within a Pacific salmon (sockeye salmon and kokanee, *Oncorhynchus nerka*). Evolution 50: 401–416.

Tiegs, S., P. Levi, J. Ruegg, D. Chaloner, J. Tank, G. Lamberti. 2011. Ecological effects of live salmon exceed those of carcasses during annual spawning migration. Ecosystems 14: 598–614.

Ueda, H., M. Kaeriyama, K. Mukasa, A. Urano, H. Kudo, T. Shoji, Y. Tokumitsu, K. Yamauchi, K. Kurihara. 1998. Lacustrine sockeye salmon return straight to their natal area from open water using both visual and olfactory cues. Chem. Senses 23: 207–212.

van den Berghe, E., M. Gross. 1984. Female size and nest depth in coho salmon *(Oncorhynchus kisutch)*. Can. J. Fish. Aquat. Sci. 41: 204–206.

Vandermeer, J. 1972. Niche theory. Annu. Rev. Ecol. Syst. 3: 107–132.

Verspoor, J., D. Braun, J. Reynolds. 2010. Quantitative links between Pacific salmon and stream periphyton. Ecosystems 13: 1020–1034.

Weber, P., I. Hutcheon, K. McKeegan, L. Ingram. 2002. Otolith sulfur isotope method to reconstruct salmon *(Oncorhynchus tshawytscha)* life history. Can. J. Fish. Aquat. Sci. 59: 587–591.

Whittaker, R., S. Levin, R. Root. 1973. Niche, habitat, and ecotope. American Naturalist 107: 321–338.

Wilkinson, C., M. Hocking, T. Reimchen. 2005. Uptake of salmon-derived nitrogen by mosses and liverworts in coastal British Columbia. Oikos 108: 85–98.

Willson, M., S. Gende, B. Marston. 1998. Fishes and the forest. BioScience 48: 455–462.

Willson, M., K. Halupka. 1995. Anadromous fish as keystone species in vertebrate communities. Conservation Biology 9: 489–497.

Wilzbach, M., B. Harvey, J. White, R. Nakamoto. 2005. Effects of riparian canopy opening and salmon carcass addition on the abundance and growth of resident salmonids. Can. J. Fish. Aquat. Sci. 62: 58–67.

Winder, M., D. Schindler, J. Moore, S. Johnson, J. Palen. 2005. Do bears facilitate transfer of salmon resources to aquatic macroinvertebrates? Can. J. Fish. Aquat. Sci. 62: 2285–2293.

Wipfli, M., J. Hudson, J. Caouette. 2004. Restoring productivity of salmon-based food webs: Contrasting effects of salmon carcass and salmon carcass analog additions on stream-resident salmonids. Trans. Am. Fish. Soc. 133: 1440–1454.

Wipfli, M., J. Hudson, J. Caouette, D. Chaloner. 2003. Marine subsidies in freshwater ecosystems: Salmon carcasses increase growth rates of stream-resident salmonids. Trans. Am. Fish. Soc. 132: 371–381.

University of California Press, one of the most distinguished university presses in the United States, enriches lives around the world by advancing scholarship in the humanities, social sciences, and natural sciences. Its activities are supported by the UC Press Foundation and by philanthropic contributions from individuals and institutions. For more information, visit www.ucpress.edu.

University of California Press
Berkeley and Los Angeles, California

University of California Press, Ltd.
London, England

Library of Congress Cataloging-in-Publication Data

Stokes, M. Dale (Malcolm Dale), 1967– author.
    The fish in the forest : salmon and the web of life / Dale Stokes ; photographs by Doc White.
        pages   cm
    Includes bibliographical references.
    ISBN 978-0-520-26920-0 (cloth : alk. paper)
    1. Pacific salmon—Ecology—North Pacific Ocean.   2. Pacific salmon—Ecology—Northwest, Pacific.   I. White, Doc, 1946– illustrator.   II. Title.
    QL638.S2.S845 2014   2014
    597.5' 6—dc23

                                        2013033773

Manufactured in China

23   22   21   20   19   18   17   16   15   14
10   9   8   7   6   5   4   3   2   1

The paper used in this publication meets the minimum requirements of ANSI/NISO z39.48–1992 (R 2002) *(Permanence of Paper)*.

DESIGNER Claudia Smelser
TEXT 10.5/16 Miller Text
DISPLAY Proxima Nova
COMPOSITOR BookMatters, Berkeley
PREPRESS Embassy Graphics
PRINTER AND BINDER QuaLibre